AF600624

THE CATHOLIC UNIVERSITY OF AMERICA
CANON LAW STUDIES
Number 102

THE SIMPLE CONVALIDATION OF MARRIAGE

AN HISTORICAL SYNOPSIS AND COMMENTARY

A DISSERTATION

Submitted to the Faculty of Canon Law of the Catholic University of America in Partial Fulfillment of the Requirements for the Degree of

DOCTOR OF CANON LAW

BY

REV. JAMES H. BRENNAN, M. A., S. T. B., J. C. L.
Priest of St. Sulpice

THE CATHOLIC UNIVERSITY OF AMERICA
WASHINGTON, D. C.
1937

Nihil Obstat:

VALENTINUS T. SCHAAF, O. F. M., J. C. D.,
Censor Deputatus.

Washingtonii, die XI Maii, 1937.

Imprimatur:

MICHAEL J. CURLEY, D. D.,
Archiepiscopus Baltimorensis.

Baltimorae, die XI Maii, 1937.

PRINTED IN THE UNITED STATES OF AMERICA
BY J. H. FURST COMPANY, BALTIMORE, MARYLAND

TO

FATHER C. V. O'BRIEN

IN GRATITUDE

TABLE OF CONTENTS

FOREWORD

In theory invalid marriages admit of four solutions. The parties involved may be permitted to cohabit in good faith, to live together as brother and sister, to seek a declaration of nullity, or to convadidate their invalid union. In practice convalidation usually is the most convenient and satisfactory method of rectifying invalid marriages. In the majority of instances simple convalidation should be preferred to the extraordinary *sanatio,* it is less troublesome and more rapid in achieving satisfactory results.

The Canon Law which regulates and governs simple convalidation is explained in the following pages with a view to overcome the major practical difficulties incidental to its use. The plan includes a treatment of the nature and historical development, a discussion of the essential elements and the manner in which marriages are convalidated according to the source of their invalidity. Through it all there has been an attempt to distinguish clearly and carefully between the simple and the extraordinary methods. Finally a chapter has been added dealing with American Civil Law because of its importance in the marriages of unbaptized persons.

It gives the author pleasure to express publicly his genuine gratitude to each and all who helped to bring the work to its completion. He is sincerely thankful to the members of the Faculty of the School of Canon Law at the Catholic University. He wishes finally to acknowledge with gratitude the gracious aid and courtesy extended by the librarians at the Catholic University.

THE SIMPLE CONVALIDATION OF MARRIAGE

CHAPTER I

NATURE OF SIMPLE CONVALIDATION

Convalidation is a remedy of law by which an act that has been null and void is made valid. In Canon Law an act is null when "it lacks those things that essentially constitute it, or the solemnities or conditions which the sacred canons require under pain of invalidity."[1] Validity therefore depends upon the presence of certain essential facts and indispensable conditions prescribed by the nature of the act or law. If these facts are present and the conditions verified the act is valid; if they are absent, it is invalid. Upon this alone does validity depend. It is something objective. Hence it matters not if the persons concerned are aware or not of the presence or the absence of these essential requisites; such knowledge has no bearing upon the objective validity of the act. Nor does it matter how long the act remains invalid, the mere passing of time in itself will not validate an invalid act.[2] Only by supplying for the essential deficiencies, by complying with the prescribed solemnities or by fulfilling the requisite conditions does it become valid. This act of supplying later what was wanting the first time the act was performed is called convalidation.

The term "convalidation" is preferred to "validation." At first sight the latter term may seem more apt because it is a question here of conferring validity upon an act that had at no time been valid. Convalidation is chosen however because it connotes the validating of an act that had some appearance of validity the first time it was performed. This appearance of validity is always required in some form before the term convalidation may be used. If an act were manifestly and evidently invalid from the beginning it can scarcely be said to be convalidated at least in the strict meaning of the word. In this general sense the term has several uses in Canon Law. It is applied not only to the marriage contract but to other phases of legislation as well. Thus Canon 586 of the

[1] Canon 1680.

[2] "Non firmatur tractu temporis quod de jure ab initio non subsistit." Reg. 17, R. J. in VI°.

Code admits its use in the matter of religious profession; Canon 150 denies its use in the provision of ecclesiastical offices.

Applied to marriage convalidation may be defined as an act by which a marriage, null from the beginning, is now rendered valid.[3] It implies that the marriage is contracted over again, that consent is exchanged anew, but this time all the essentials necessary for validity are present. The first time the ceremony was performed it was neither true sacrament nor contract but now, at the second ceremony, it begins to be both and obtains the effects of both as it would have obtained them from the beginning had it been valid. In a strict sense marriage can be said to be convalidated only when it had some appearance of validity in the first celebration. The "*species matrimonii*" that is, the external form prescribed by law, must have been observed.[4] Thus a sinful or concubinary union resulting from an attempted marriage by two Catholics before a civil officer cannot be convalidated in the strict meaning of that term, because these attempts do not have the appearance of validity. Any subsequent marriage entered into by people living in such a union would be their first marriage. But in a broader sense convalidation includes all invalid unions even those that very evidently lack the appearance of marriage. When used in its strict meaning convalidation has its proper place in putative marriages in which one or both parties have no knowledge of the invalidity of their marriage.[5]

The Code divides convalidation into two classes, simple and extraordinary (*sanatio in radice*). The former is not defined explicitly by the Code but its definition may be gathered from the canons which treat of the manner in which it is to be effected.[6] Simple convalidation is an act by which a marriage that has been null and void from the beginning is rendered valid by the renewal of consent. It presupposes the removal of the cause of the invalidity. The removal qualifies the persons to make a valid act of consent; the renewal itself effects the convalidation. For example, the marriage of two Catholics is invalidated by the impediment of affinity. Now they desire to convalidate it. They must apply for

[3] Gasparri, *De Matrimonio* (Ed. 1932), n. 1186.

[4] O'Neill, *Extent of Guarantees in Mixed Marriages—IER*, XXIII (1924), 417, 2.

[5] Canon 1015, § 4.

[6] Canons 1133-1137.

a dispensation from the impediment and having received it they are qualified to renew consent validly and thus effect a valid marriage. They actually contract it at the moment of renewal of consent.

Extraordinary convalidation (*sanatio in radice*) is defined as the "convalidation of marriage which imports besides a dispensation or cessation of the impediment, a dispensation also from the renewal of consent; and by a fiction of the law it supplies a retroactive validity to the canonical effects of the marriage so that they are reckoned to be the same as though the marriage had been valid from the beginning."[7]

The comparison of these two definitions reveals two very marked and important differences. They concern the renewal of consent and the effects they produce. In simple convalidation renewal of consent is absolutely essential to validity, in the *sanatio* the renewal is not necessary. The whole simple convalidation will have no effect whatever if the renewal is omitted; in fact the two acts are practically identified, one cannot exist without the other. The renewal may take place explicitly or implicitly by words or by actions, but it must be made in some manner, for it is indispensable to simple convalidation. On the contrary it is not required in the *sanatio,* but it is dispensed from by the law itself either because it is impossible to obtain it or because the parties are unwilling or unable to give it. By the very fact that the *sanatio* is granted the dispensation from the renewal of consent is granted with it. Thus it follows that the *sanatio* can be effective even without the cooperation of the parties themselves, and its effectiveness depends primarily upon the authority who issues it.[8] But simple convalidation imports the cooperation of the parties and the validity of the marriage depends primarily upon their act of consent. The contrast between these two methods of convalidation is sharpened by an example. Two persons have contracted a marriage that is invalid due to the impediment of consanguinity. In either method a dispensation from the impediment is necessary. If the simple method on convalidation is employed the parties must give an

[7] Canon 1138.

[8] This is exemplified in a general *sanatio* which is granted to convalidate many marriages at one time. Cf. S. C. S. Off., *Coreae*, Sept. 11, 1878, ad. 1—*Coll.*, n. 1499; S. C. Prop. Fide, *Sutchuen.*, Jan. 17, 1836, ad 1—*Coll.*, n. 845; *Yun-Nan*, June 1, 1845—*Coll.*, n. 995.

entirely new act of consent after the impediment has been removed by a dispensation, and they must give that consent with the knowledge that their marriage was invalid. But if one of the parties refuses to renew consent and if he does not retract the consent he formerly gave, the other may ask for a *sanatio,* which will dispense from the necessity of renewing consent and at the same time remove the impediment.

A second important distinction between the two concerns the effects that follow from them. First they differ in the time at which these effects begin to exist. A *sanatio* renders a marriage valid and takes effect at the time it is granted by the superior; even though at that moment the parties are not aware of the granting of the *sanatio.* But in the simple convalidation the effects begin to exist only at the moment in which consent is renewed and united to the consent of the other party, whose consent may also have been renewed or was at least still persevering. Secondly, the extent of the effects is also different. The *sanatio* by a fiction of law renders the effects of the marriage juridically valid from the very beginning, that is, from the time of the first ceremony or when the consent was first exchanged. It does not of course validate the marriage itself from that time so that the period during which the marriage was invalid is completely erased by the granting of the *sanatio.* To maintain this would involve a contradiction that is absurd. The effects which are referred to are the canonical effects, and especially the legitimation of children. Simple convalidation includes no such retroactive power; the effects of the marriage are validated only from the time that consent is renewed. A marriage, for example, has been invalid for ten years and during that time four children have been born. If the union is validated by the mere renewal of consent the marriage becomes valid and the children legitimate only from the moment of renewal. During the ten previous years they have been illegitimate and, for all that concerns those ten years, they will always be considered illegitimate. On the contrary, if the invalid marriage is validated by a *sanatio* the union is made valid both as a sacrament and as contract from the moment in which the *sanatio* is granted. But the effects enjoy a greater privilege. They are validated in such a manner that they are considered to have been valid even during the ten years previous. The children in this event are considered (as far as the canonical effects are concerned) to be legitimate and to obtain the same status in law in the same manner as those who are born of a marriage which was valid from the beginning.

It is well to note that both of these methods can be employed to convalidate not only individual invalid marriages but also many marriages at the same time. It may happen that a large number of marriages in a certain country are invalid because they have been contracted in general ignorance of an ecclesiastical law. For such a situation either remedy may be used. The parties to each marriage may be asked to renew their consent after having been told that the union is invalid; or the authorities may grant a general *sanatio* to effectuate the validation of all the marriages without any renewal of consent or knowledge of the nullity of the previous union. It is to be expected that the latter method will be used because it is more convenient and more sure of attaining the desired results. Thus the Constitution *Provida* of Pius X under date of June 13, 1906,[9] convalidated by means of the *sanatio* all mixed marriages in Germany that had been invalid because of lack of form.

Simple convalidation itself may be distinguished into two classes, convalidation by natural law or by ecclesiastical law. Each is distinct from the other and each has its own peculiar and important consequences. The difference consists precisely in this that ecclesiastical law always demands a renewal of consent and knowledge of the nullity of the former union. Natural law on the contrary does not require either of these elements; for its effectiveness the mere perseverance of consent suffices and is effective to convalidate a marriage when the obstacle to validity has been removed. It is necessary of course that such consent persevere otherwise there can be no marriage for even natural law demands consent to effect the marriage contract. But assuming that it does endure there is no need to renew it. For example, a marriage between two non-baptized persons is invalid because one of the parties is already married. The impediment of *ligamen* being of natural law renders such a union invalid. But the first marriage is dissolved by the death of the other partner to it. In this event the second marriage now becomes valid if consent perseveres, because the impedi-

[9] *ASS*, XXXIX (1906), pp. 81 ff.

ment of *ligamen* has been removed and the naturally valid consent which was formerly given becomes effective at the moment in which the impediment has been removed. But if these two persons were baptized they would be under the necessity of renewing consent because their convalidation must be effected in accord with ecclesiastical law which demands renewal of consent. Their marriage remains invalid until they do renew consent, even though their consent given at the time they entered marriage actually perseveres.

Convalidation must not be confused with ratification of marriage. The latter term may be used to signify two distinct processes, each of which differs from convalidation. To ratify a marriage may mean to make it licit; for example, a Catholic marries a baptized non-Catholic validly but not licitly because he has neglected to obtain the proper dispensation from mixed religion. In this case the marriage is illicit and if later on it is made licit it is said to be ratified. Or again to ratify a marriage may mean to sacramentalize it in this sense that a valid non-sacramental marriage may become a sacrament if the parties or party as the case may be receive baptism and thus become capable of a sacramental marriage. Thus if two persons who are not baptized contract a valid legitimate marriage (*matrimonium legitimum*) their union is not sacramental because they are not capable of receiving the sacraments. If later they receive the sacrament of baptism it renders them qualified to receive also the sacrament of matrimony and their marriage as a result becomes sacramental. Neither of these can be identified with convalidation. The latter has to do only with invalid marriages, while both the former are concerned with marriages that are already valid. The changes which were effected after the marriages had been contracted did not affect the validity.

Finally convalidation is not the same as a marriage that becomes valid when a condition upon which consent depends is fulfilled. When a future licit condition is attached to the matrimonial consent it suspends the effect of the consent until the condition is verified. If it is verified the consent becomes absolute and effective, and therefore the marriage becomes valid. But until that time no marriage exists not even what might be called an invalid marriage. The parties to it know well that their union is only conditional and do not make any pretense to married life until the condition is fulfilled. Their consent is valid but ineffective because it is suspended. When the consent has been freed of the condition it takes its effect immediately; there is no need for a new act of consent to validate the marriage. But in convalidation the marriage is not merely suspended it is invalid; the consent can never take its effect until it is renewed, for it is not dependent upon a condition for its efficacy but upon the removal of an obstacle to its validity and further upon the renewal required by ecclesiastical law.

CHAPTER II

HISTORY OF SIMPLE CONVALIDATION

Article I

Convalidation in Roman Law

The Roman law sources contain no definite treatise on the convalidation of marriage. They do not even employ the words valid or invalid in connection with the marriage contract. The usual classification is twofold, *matrimonium justum* and *matrimonium injustum.*[1] The *matrimonium injustum* is also called *matrimonium non legitimum.*[2] All these terms take their meaning from the relation of the individual marriage to the law. Those which are contracted by people with full capacity for marriage and which are entirely legal in all their aspects are termed *justa matrimonia* or *justae nuptiae.*

If the law was observed in its entirety and if the parties themselves possessed all the capacities required by Roman law they contracted a valid marriage, and all the consequences, v. g., the citizenship of the offspring, would follow from it.[3] If the prescriptions of the law were not observed or if the parties did not have the capacity to marry, their union was termed a *matrimonium injustum.* The capacity to marry might be given as a right, as in the case of a Roman citizen; or it might have been conceded as a privilege either to the person as an individual or as a member of a community. In either case it allowed the persons so privileged to contract *justae nuptiae.*[4] Even a Roman or one who had the capacity of marriage could contract an unjust marriage if he should attempt marriage against the provisions of the law. Thus, for instance, there were certain classes prohibited from intermarrying, e. g., senators and freedwomen, tutors and wards, ancestors and descendants.[5] Yet these laws were not so rigorous that they never suffered exception. Dispensations were not unknown in Roman law.

[1] D. (38.11) 1. [2] D. (50.1) 37.2. [3] G. (1.56; 67; 76).

[4] Corbett, *The Roman Law of Marriage*, pp. 102-103, 139.

[5] D. (23.2) 27; (23.2) 59; 60; G. (1.59).

As with convalidation, so there is no special treatise upon the theory of dispensations, no peculiar section of the sources is devoted to it. Yet in fact, dispensations, considered as relaxations of the law, did exist.[6] Since this is so, it may easily be concluded that dispensations were granted for marrying and for the convalidating of marriage which had been contracted contrary to laws.[7]

Beyond this there are fragments and laws of the sources in which the principle, if not the actual fact, of convalidation is to be found.[8] Thus a marriage between a Roman citizen and a woman who is an alien or Latin, whom the Roman believes to be a citizen, is not *justae nuptiae* because the woman lacks capacity. As a result the children born are not citizens—but they obtain the same status as the mother and are either aliens or Latins. By proving the existence of a justifiable cause for the error of the father the wife and children are made Roman citizens and the children come under the father's *potestas.* The Roman citizen had capacity for civil marriage in this instance, retroactively.[9] The same convalidating process corrects a marriage in which the woman is the Roman citizen and her husband a Latin or alien.[10]

There are in Roman law definite traces of a process which, though it is not termed convalidation by the law, is so in fact. A marriage contracted against the prohibition of the law would in some cases be null, and later could be validated by the continuance of the two people in the marriage.[11] Among the marriages that were prohibited was the union contracted between a Senator (who was actually engaged in fulfilling his duty and office) and a freedwoman. Such a marriage was null.[12] But if they continued in that union and in their marital consent after the Senator had lost his dignity and office the marriage was convalidated and they became true husband and wife.[13] Again, if a marriage was at-

[6] Cicognani, *Canon Law,* pp. 830-831.

[7] Stiegler, *Dispensation, Dispensationswesen und Dispensationsrecht,* p. 16.

[8] Roby, *Roman Private Law,* I, p. 210.

[9] Gaius (1. 67).

[10] Gaius (1. 68).

[11] Buckland, *A Text Book of Roman Law,* p. 114; Voet, *Commentarium ad Pandectas,* III, n. 39.

[12] D. (23. 2) 27.

[13] Savigny, *Zeitschrift,* XXIV (1903), 66. "Quod ergo ab initio non valet, ex postfacto convalescit"—Reg. 17, R. J., in VI°.

tempted contrary to the prohibition which forbids provincial officers from marrying a woman of the provinces, there was no valid marriage. "Nor is there any doubt of the sanction, which is nullity." [14] But if the two partners persevere in their union they will become husband and wife in valid nuptials after the officer ended his tenure of office.[15] Another example is that of the validation of an invalid union contracted between a guardian, or his son, and his former ward who was a minor at the time of the marriage. This marriage is invalid.[16] But it could be convalidated if marital consent continued in both parties after the ward reached the proper age.[17]

All these are examples of the convalidation of marriage. The unions had been null because of the prohibitions of the state but they became valid by the disappearance of the impediment and the perseverance of the first intention in the married parties. It seems clear then that the Romans did have at least the rudiments of the process of convalidation. There is no extensive legislation upon it but from the examples offered one can say that it existed in fact; the legislation is not detailed but it does contain the general principle. The manner of convalidation is not mentioned except to say that the perseverance of the parties in their first intention is necessary. They did not demand another and new consent of the parties, they considered the perseverance of the former consent sufficient to convalidate the marriage. Nor does there appear any evidence of dispensation in these cases, usually the marriage becomes valid after the impediment of its nature has disappeared. It is safe to conclude that the principle of convalidation is definitely established in Roman Law.

Article 2

To the Tenth Century

The history of legislation concerning the convalidation of marriage in the first centuries of the Church is hazy and uncertain. It is difficult to find definite and explicit traces of its existence and use. The few references that do exist are the subject of divergent

[14] Corbett, *The Roman Law of Marriage*, p. 42.

[15] D. (23. 2) 65. pr.; Voet, *Commentarium ad Pandectas*, III, n. 39.

[16] Corbett, *The Roman Law of Marriage*, p. 47.

[17] D. (23. 2) 64. 1.

conjecture and of different interpretation among canonists. From this vagueness, however, there stand out several fairly certain conclusions: first, it is to be expected that convalidation would not have been developed fully at this period; second, that the principle of dispensation to which convalidation is necessarily joined was known; third, there are evidences of the use of convalidating power though its exact nature is not determined.

It is readily understood why there should not be a fully developed legislation on convalidation in the early Church. Like all other Church discipline the marriage law was in its infancy. Many of the situations that are provided for in the codification of Gratian, of Gregory and in decrees of the later councils did not present themselves to the early Christians; indeed, they could not have easily occurred when the Church embraced but a handful of members. But the spread of Christianity and the consequent adaptation of its discipline to the nations that came into its fold gave rise to new problems and necessitated the enactment of new laws. This was true of matrimonial law as it was true of all the legislation of the Church. Hence it is to this period that we look for the first vestige of convalidation.

The first traces of convalidation appear in the sixth century. They were occasioned by the barbarian converts who embraced Christianity about that time. They could scarcely be expected to know the details of the Church's matrimonial legislation since it differed so radically from their own. The result was that many of them in ignorance of the law contracted invalid marriages. These were convalidated by the Church. The earliest examples of convalidation of marriage are found in Gaul. The very first were enacted at the Council of Agde (Agatha) in the province of Languedoc in southern Gaul. It was convoked in September, 506, by Archbishop Caesarius of Arles.[18] Seventy-one of the canons of this council were accepted as genuine by Gratian in his *Decretum* and received in almost their complete form. Among them is canon sixty-one which contains definite legislation on dispensations granted after marriage had been invalidly contracted.[19] It states that incestuous marriages already contracted invalidly will be

[18] Mansi, VIII, 335.

[19] C. 8, C. XXXV, q. 2 et 3. Freisen, *Geschichte des canonischen Eherechts*, 377.

allowed to continue without dissolution. This canon was later embodied in the canons of the Council of Epaon convoked by Sigismund of Burgundy in 517. Canon thirty forbids the marriage of two people who have an impediment of affinity; such marriages it also calls incestuous. But marriages of this kind already contracted are not to be broken.[20] The third Council of Orleans in the year 538 repeated the same legislation in canon twenty-seven.[21] And only three years later in the fourth Council of Orleans, 541, the same provision is made for marriages contracted with the impediment of affinity. They were to continue as valid.[22]

The exact nature of these dispensations has been the subject of lively discussion among canonists. That the impediment was a diriment impediment and hence that the marriages referred to were invalid seems to be agreed upon by most of them.[23] The difficulty arises when they seek to explain the manner in which this convalidation was effected. Was it a real convalidation? If so, was it simple or extraordinary? The best opinion seems to be that these enactments were true convalidations and that they were simple convalidations. That they were genuine convalidations of invalid marriages is generally admitted and seems to be proved by the fact that the impediments in the cases were diriment. Some authors find in them the first traces of the extraordinary method of convalidation.[24] Evidently the basis for this assertion is the fact that the canons say nothing about the renewal of consent which regularly is demanded by ecclesiastical law in ordinary convalidation. But it is not necessary to admit that they were extraordinary merely because the renewal of consent was not asked. The actual cohabitation of the parties could be understood as a sign of the perseverance of their first consent and would be sufficient to make the marriage valid after the impediment had been removed. Explicit renewal of consent was not required by ecclesiastical law until the

[20] Mansi, VIII, 562-3. [21] Mansi, IX, 14-15. [22] Mansi, IX, 118.

[23] Pirhing, *Jus Canonicum*, IV, Tit. XIV, cap. 2, p. 114, no. 32; Reiffenstuel, IV, Tit. 14, no. 49; Laymann, *Theologia Moralis*, V, Tr. 10, par 4, c. 6, no. 6; Gonzales, *Commentaria Perpetua In Singulos Textus Quinque Librorum Decretalium*, n. 11, on c. 5. X. *De Consang Et Affin*, IV, 14; Sanchez, *De Matrimonio*, VII, Disp. 65, n. 5.

[24] Perrone, *De Matrimonio Christiano*, II, p. 153; Giovine, *De Dispensationibus Matrimonialibus*, I, p. 598.

thirteenth century.[25] Beyond this, the common opinion seems to be that the extraordinary method of convalidation came into existence only in the fourteenth century when Boniface VIII granted such a *sanatio* to Queen Mary, wife of King Sancho of Castile, in 1301.[26] It would seem only reasonable then to conclude that these are examples of the simple method of convalidation.[27] This conclusion is strengthened by the fact that the principle of convalidation was known and used in Roman Law.

Between the sixth and the tenth centuries there are isolated instances of the use of the simple convalidation of marriage. During the eighth century two councils adopt the stand of the councils of the sixth century. Canon I of the Council of Verberie, 753, limits the dispensation to the fourth degree, but does not separate those who had contracted the marriage before with the impediment.[28] The Council of Compiegne, 756 or 757, permitted those who had been joined in invalid marriages to remain in them if the impediment was of the fourth degree; but if in the third the parties had to be separated.[29] The repetition found during the ninth century leads one to conclude that convalidation had become a firmly established plan in the Church's legislation. Thus the Council of Worms, 868,[30] and the council of Doucy, 874,[31] repeated the same legislation as is found in the earlier councils.

From what has been noted in this first period there is no doubt that the dispensations were granted, and granted after the marriages had been invalidly contracted. From this it follows that there was convalidation of some kind though its exact nature is difficult to determine. It may have been of the nature of a *sanatio in radice* though in view of the fact that *sanationes* very probably began only in the fourteenth century that is not probable. Finally and more correctly it was simple convalidation without the

[25] Scherer, *Handbuch des Kirchenrechts*, II, 501; Wernz, *Jus Decretalium*, IV, n. 610, note 20.

[26] Rigantius, *Commentaria*, Reg. 49, p. 7.

[27] Stiegler, *Dispensation, Dispensationswesen, und Dispensationsrecht*, p. 70.

[28] Harduinus, III, 1990; Hefele, *Histoire des Conciles*, III, par. 2, 941.

[29] Hefele, III, par. 2, 918.

[30] C. 32—Mansi, XV, 875.

[31] Mansi XVII A, 282; Hefele, IV, 370.

obligation of renewing consent which was not introduced until the thirteenth century. In any case these examples supply us with the origin of all convalidation in marriage law.

Article 3

To the Council of Trent

At the end of the tenth century a change is noted in the manner of granting dispensations to convalidate marriage. Hitherto the dispensation had always been granted for general convalidations and for the reason of public welfare. But now the practice of conceding dispensations in particular cases was introduced, either for the private good of the parties or for the general welfare of the countries, as happens often in the case of rulers.[32]

The first example of this new form of dispensation seems to have been granted in the year 990 to William, Duke of Astarac, by Bishop Garcias of Auch. The Duke, against the wishes of the Bishop, had married a woman related to him within the forbidden degrees of consanguinity. He persisted in his invalid union and no amount of persuasion or threat could induce him to separate from the woman who he knew was not his wife. When the Bishop realized this he granted the Duke a dispensation by which he could convalidate the marriage. This example is important not only because it was the first in individual cases but also because it was the first granted by a bishop.[33] Now that the Church had begun this new practice it may be expected that she had opened the way for the convalidation of many invalid marriages. The number and the extent of impediments during these centuries made it very easy to contract an invalid marriage in good faith. Thus, for instance, the impediment of consanguinity could be contracted by those related in the seventh degree.[34]

In the year 1013 the marriage of Antonius Hainerius of Hanover and the daughter of Count Herman, a relative within the forbidden degree of consanguinity was convalidated after Bishop Gerard of Cambrai had granted the dispensation for convalida-

[32] Brys, *De Dispensatione in Jure Canonico, Praenotanda*, p. 10; p. 62.

[33] Stiegler, *Dispensation, Dispensationswesen und Dispensationsrecht*, p. 245; *Gallia Christiana*, I, 978; App. 159.

[34] Council of Rome (1063), c. 9—Mansi, XIX, 1026.

tion. The motive was the peace the convalidation insured.[35] Archbishop Poppo of Trier granted a dispensation in 1036 to the lawyer Theofried to make possible the validation of his marriage which had been invalid because of the consanguinity in the fifth and sixth degrees. The Archbishop, who had in the beginning refused the dispensation, granted it with the hope that it would avert a threatened scandal.[36] In 1043 the Abbot Siegfried of Goize convalidated the disputed marriage of Henry III and Agnes of Poitou which had been invalid because of consanguinity in the fourth degree.[37]

A very famous example of convalidation occurred in the year 1059, during the pontificate of Pope Nicolas II (1058-1061). Mathilda, the daughter of Baldwin of Flanders, had contracted an invalid marriage with William, Duke of Normandy, who was related to her in the third degree of consanguinity. The marriage had been forbidden by the Council of Rheims and also by Pope Leo IX who had convalidated her father's marriage. In spite of the prohibition the marriage was contracted. As a result, Normandy was placed under an interdict. This evidently would have had the desired result—the separation of the two persons—but such a separation would have brought war between Normandy and Flanders. Lanfranc, afterwards Archbishop of Canterbury, who was on a mission to Rome in connection with the heresy of Berengarius, petitioned the Pope to convalidate the marriage in order to avert the war. In 1059 the Pope granted the dispensation with the condition that each of the two should build a monastery. The monasteries were actually built in Caen, a city of Normandy.[38]

A strange case comes to notice during the pontificate of Gregory VII (1075-1085). William, Bishop of Padua, had assisted at the marriage of his sister, Mathilda, to Count Azzo of Este, although he knew there were present two diriment impediments, consanguinity

[35] Lupus, *Synodorum Generalium et Provincialium Decreta et Canones*, IV, p. 189.

[36] Stiegler, *Dispensation, Dispensationswesen und Dispensationsrecht*, p. 258.

[37] Stiegler, *ibid.*, pp. 260, 261.

[38] Lupus, *Synodorum Generalium et Provincialium Decreta et Canones*, IV, 189; Thomassin, *Vetus et Nova Ecclesiae Disciplina*, II, Lib. III, cap. 29, n. 10; Rigantius, *Commentaria*, II, Reg. 49, n. 8.

and affinity. When knowledge of this was brought to the attention of Pope Gregory, instead of separating them, he allowed them to live together but with the condition they would not use their marriage rights until they had first obtained his permission. There is no evidence that he did actually grant a convalidation but it is evident that he foresaw the possibility of granting one.[39]

The frequency of convalidations in the eleventh century was continued and increased in the twelfth. The first that comes to notice was granted by Pope Pascal II (1099-1118) to King Boleslaus III of Poland. He had contracted an invalid marriage with Zbyslawa, a relative in the fourth degree.[40] Three years later the same Pope was confronted with a situation similar to that of Nicolas II and the Duke of Normandy. The marriage of Philip I, King of France, and Bertrada of Montfort had been declared invalid by the synod of Poitiers because there was present an impediment of consanguinity. The same council threatened excommunication and interdict unless the two separated. They promised in the Council of Paris (1105) to separate and later actually separated. They applied to the Pope for a dispensation. It was granted and their marriage was convalidated in 1106.[41] The increased frequency with which dispensations were granted during the twelfth century may explain why the *post factum* dispensation, which hitherto had been granted only where there was an impediment of affinity or consanguinity was now extended to other impediments. During the pontificate of Alexander III a marriage could be convalidated if it had been null because of *ligamen*. This was allowed after the death of the first wife. It was necessary that the second wife should have been ignorant of the impediment when she entered into the bigamous marriage.[42] During the pontificate of Lucius III (1181-1185) convalidation was permitted in the case of a marriage null because of the impediment of abduction. In this case it was necessary that the woman should freely consent to marry her abductor. After the duress was removed and she had moved to a place of safety and freedom.[43] Clement III (1187-

[39] Jaffe, *Regesta Pontificum Romanorum*, R. 4834.

[40] Rigantius, *Commentaria*, II, Reg. 49, n. 6.

[41] Rigantius, *Commentaria*, II, Reg. 49, n. 6.

[42] C. I, X, *qui matrimonium accusare possunt*, IV, 18.

[43] Rigantius, *Commentaria*, II, Reg. 49, nn. 76 ff.

1191) allowed the convalidation of a marriage where there had been no consent given because violence had been present in the first ceremony.[44]

Although there was a decided and very noticeable increase in the number of convalidations during this period there was also a number of cases in which the petition was refused. Thus Pope Alexander II (1061-1073) said that he lacked the authority to grant such dispensations. This was in reply to a request of the Bishop of Venice for a dispensation from affinity so that two of his subjects might validate their marriage.[45] Gregory VII (1073-1085) refused two such petitions for dispensations to convalidate invalid marriages. He ordered Robert, King of France, to separate from his wife because they had been invalidly married while an impediment of spiritual relationship existed between them. Robert afterward married another woman.[46] The Pope's legate, Cardinal Otto, had insisted in synod that the Emperor Hermanus should separate from his illegally married wife.[47]

It is necessary to refer here to dissimulation. It is defined as a juridic connivance at an invalid act. At times it is not expedient to reveal the invalidity of an act, or it may be possible to remove it. In such cases the superior assumes a passive attitude and does nothing. He allows the act to continue. Such dissimulation on the part of the superior supposes good faith in the parties concerned, and they are allowed to continue in this good faith, especially when it is foreseen that scandal or embarrassment will arise from the revelation of the invalidity of their marriage.[48]

This is dissimulation as it is known today in law. But formerly, very often it was not merely passive permission for invalidly married people to live together, but also a true dispensation from the impediment. At least this was the more common opinion. It is then closely linked with the process of convalidation of marriages.[49]

[44] C. 4, X, *qui matrimonium accusare possunt,* IV, 18.

[45] Lupus, *Decreta,* IV, p. 188.

[46] Rigantius, *Commentaria,* II, Reg. 49, n. 5.

[47] Lupus, *Decreta,* IV, 188.

[48] Cicognani (Brennan-O'Hara), *Canon Law,* p. 832, 833; Wernz-Vidal, *Jus Canonicum,* V, n. 651.

[49] C. 6, X, *de consanguinitate et affinitate,* IV, 14; *Instructio Cardinalis*

It was late in the thirteenth century when the renewal of consent was demanded for the first time in the simple convalidation of marriage. It was a distinct innovation in the practice of the simple convalidation. The early councils, as noted before, merely issued permission to those living in invalid marriages to continue in them. They did not require a renewal of consent. In the tenth century when the practice was extended to individual marriages there is still no mention of the renewal of consent.[50] No evidence has thus far appeared to prove that it was demanded before the thirteenth century. It seems only reasonable to conclude that had it been required it would have been noticed in some of the documents of the time. In the year 1281 there is clear and explicit evidence of the demand for the renewal of consent. On September 5 of that year a rescript of the Sacred Penitentiary contains the instructions "postquam de novo consenserint." And just two years previous to this a rescript of the same tribunal in similar matter did not contain that phrase. The earlier rescript merely stated "*Quod impedimento non obstante in hoc contracto matrimonio permanere possitis.*"[51] Shortly after, in the year 1288, in a rescript of March 6, the Sacred Penitentiary does not use these words in dispensing from consanguinity in the fourth degree.[52] It is difficult to conclude from these rescripts that the practice was universal and binding. Nor can it safely be concluded that the practice began exactly at this period. Probably it did. And the reason why the renewal of consent was not required in the last of these rescripts may be that the impediment was occult, at least in fact even if public by its nature; while in the former rescript the impediment was public. The renewal of consent when there was a question of an occult impediment was not the subject of universal agreement even until the new Code. The view which distinguished the two kinds of impediments and assigns that distinction as the reason for the difference in the rescript may find additional strength in the fact that previous to the council of Trent the renewal of consent was

Caprara, Par. I, n. 3—Zitelli, *De Dispensationibus Matrimonialibus*, App. p. 175, n. VI; Wernz-Vidal, *Jus Canonicum*, V, n. 651, note 3.

[50] Rigantius, *Commentaria*, II, Reg. 49, nn. 6, 7.

[51] Eubel, "Der Register Band des Cardinalgrosspoenitentiars Bentevenga,"—*AKKR*, LXIV (1890), 63, 64.

[52] *Op. cit.*, 65.

usually not necessary in dispensations that were granted by the Sacred Penitentiary. In dispensations granted before the Council of Trent from the impediment of affinity arising from illicit *copula,* there was no clause demanding a new consent.[53] It is found that as far as the fifteenth century voluntary cohabitation or the voluntary use of the marriage right was considered sufficient to convalidate a marriage. It was equivalent to consent in a marriage where the impediment had now ceased or where consent had been lacking.[54] But it must be said that in general there was no uniform practice about renewing consent until the Council of Trent, although from the fifteenth century on there is an appreciable insistence upon the renewal. But only after the Council of Trent is there anything like a uniform practice.[55]

During the fourteenth century simple and extraordinary convalidation were clearly distinguished for the first time. At almost the same time two extraordinary convalidations were granted by Boniface VIII in the year 1301. The first was conceded to Mary, the queen wife of Sancho IV, King of Castile, who had died a short time before. Their marriage had been invalidly contracted and had continued to be invalid all during the lifetime of Sancho. A number of impediments had been found, consanguinity in the third degree, affinity in the third degree *ex copula illicita,* spiritual relationship which the Queen had contracted when she had been sponsor to the child born of the illicit intercourse. When Sancho died his son Ferdinand succeeded him to the throne. It was then his mother asked the Pope for convalidation of the marriage so that her son would be considered legitimate. Her request was granted by Boniface in 1301. This was of course only an imperfect *sanatio* because it extended only to the effects of the marriage and not to the marriage itself. Nevertheless it marked for the first time a distinct departure from the discipline of the earlier centuries.[56] The second extraordinary convalidation was granted by the same Pope to Ildephonse, King of Portugal.[57] His marriage

[53] Navarrus, IV, Consil. 14, *De Sponsalibus,* n. 4.

[54] Nicolo de Tudeschi (Abbas Panormitanus), *Commentarium,* IV, De Spons., Cap. IV, n. 3; Cap. XIII, n. 6; Cap. XXIV, nn. 4 and 5.

[55] Scherer, *Handbuch des Kirchenrechtes,* II, p. 454.

[56] Rigantius, *Commentaria,* II, Reg. 49, n. 11; Mariana, *Historia General de España,* IV, p. 29.

[57] Rigantius, *Commentaria,* II, Reg. 49, n. 11.

to a countess of Poland had been invalid because of the impediment of consanguinity. It was later convalidated by a dispensation. In this case the extraordinary convalidation was perfect because it convalidated not only the effects of the marriage but also the marriage itself and the parties were not required to renew their consent.

In the beginning of this period there was an increase in the number of dispensations for the convalidation of invalid marriages.[58] This evident increase had a salutary influence upon the fathers of the Council of Trent, who, as shall be noticed in the following chapter, voted to curtail strictly the dispensations both to contract and to convalidate marriages.[59]

ARTICLE 3

To the Code of Canon Law

At the end of the last article it was noticed that the bishops came to the Council of Trent with a definite purpose of curtailing marriage dispensations. For the purpose of the present paper it will be necessary to notice several reforms which affect the simple convalidation of marriage: the restriction of impediments, the legislation on the form, and the curtailing of dispensations. Because of the multiplicity and the extent of the impediments many marriages were contracted invalidly, but in good faith, by parties who were entirely ignorant of the fact that an impediment existed in their case. This was easily possible when one remembers the extent and manner of contracting such impediments as affinity, consanguinity, spiritual relationship, public propriety. The first concern of the bishops in their reform of matrimony was to abolish or restrict the more extensive complications of the marriage impediments. Thus in the second chapter of the twenty-fourth session, *De Reformatione matrimonii,* the whole marriage legislation is prefaced by the remark: "Experience teaches that because of the multitude of prohibitions, many marriages are contracted, unknowingly at times, in these prohibited cases and the parties continue to

[58] During the Pontificate of Pope John XXII (1316-1334) over four hundred dispensations *ad convalidandum* were granted by this zealous pontiff. Cf. Mollat, *Lettres Communes des Papes D'Avignon* (Paris, 1935), John XXII; XIV vols.

[59] Sessio XXIV, *De Reformatione Matrimonii,* Cap. 5.

live in these marriages not without great sin, or the marriages are dissolved but not without grave scandal." As a result, the impediment of affinity from unlawful intercourse was limited to the first and second degree;[60] and that of public propriety arising from valid espousals was limited to the first degree.[61] Likewise restricted was the impediment of spiritual relationship. It was incurred by the baptized with the minister and sponsors, and by the baptized person's parents and the minister and sponsors.[62] A direct result of these reforms was to lessen the possibilities for invalid marriages.

Now that the likelihood of invalidity was considerably lessened the council set about to deter those people who would knowingly try to contract an invalid marriage. To this end they enacted a more rigorous and strict legislation governing the granting of dispensations for convalidation. They directed Chapter V of the Twenty-fourth session to this end. Persons who contracted marriage knowing that it would be invalid must be separated and be without any hope of obtaining a dispensation from the impediment. This applied especially to those marriages which had been not only attempted but also consummated. If the marriage had been attempted in ignorance of the impediment but with wilful neglect of the solemnities prescribed by the law the same penalty is incurred. But in the event that a marriage had been contracted with the proper solemnity, and afterwards a secret impediment was brought to the notice of the parties or the ecclesiastical authorities, a dispensation from the impediment could be given and the parties allowed to renew their consent and effect a valid marriage.[63]

Theoretically these decrees should have entirely accomplished their purpose. But in the period following the Reformation it was difficult to reduce these laws to practice. Their enforcement was not rigorous enough to obtain the desired results. The confusion following the decree *Tametsi*, the intermingling of Catholics with heretics, the intermarriage between those who were faithful to the old religion and those who had embraced the new, necessitated a mitigation of the rigor of the decrees and considerably weakened

[60] Sess. XXIV, *De Reformatione Matrimonii*, Cap. IV.
[61] Sess. XXIV, *De Reformatione Matrimonii*, Cap. III.
[62] Sess. XXIV, *De Reformatione Matrimonii*, Cap. II.
[63] Sess. XXIV, *De Reformatione Matrimonii*, Cap. V.

their force. Unless there was some manner of returning to the faith by a righting of that which was wrong, those who contracted invalid marriages might be lost to the Church altogether. Hence it is that there was a gradual return to the former more merciful discipline of dispensations after marriage. The decrees of the Council of Trent were so far relaxed in this matter that soon dispensations were granted not only when the parties were in good faith but also when they had contracted in bad faith.[64] The number of marriages invalid because of a diriment impediment was indeed lessened by the relaxations of the Council of Trent. But there was a sharp increase in the number of invalid marriages occasioned by the neglect of the new substantial form required under pain of the invalidity of the marriage. It was published in the decree *Tametsi.*[65] Before the Council of Trent no form had been prescribed for the universal church under pain of invalidity. From the very first centuries of the Church the public celebration of marriage had been enjoined and clandestine marriages had been forbidden but not under pain of being invalid.[66] Even the Fourth Lateran Council in its legislation against clandestine marriages had forbidden them merely as unlawful.[67] But the Council of Trent prescribed a new form for the celebration of marriage and proscribed clandestine marriages under pain of nullity.

> Qui aliter, quam praesenti parocho, vel alio sacerdote de ipsius parochi vel ordinarii licentia, et duobus vel tribus testibus, matrimonium contrahere attentabunt, eos sancta synodus ad sic contrahendum omnino inhabiles reddit, et hujus modi contractus irritos et nullos esse decernit, prout eos praesenti decreto irritos facit et annullat.[68]

The Fathers of the Council intended to bind subjects of the Church to this prescribed form under a very grave sanction—the invalidity of the marriage. Such was the intention, but in fact the measure was less rigorous and strict. Much of the expected reform it was calculated to achieve was frustrated by the circumstance of

[64] Wernz-Vidal, *Jus Canonicum*, n. 432, note 113; Scherer, *Handbuch des Kirchenrechts*, II, p. 466.

[65] Sess. XXIV, *De Reformatione Matrimonii*, Cap. 1.

[66] Wernz, *Jus Decretalium*, IV, nn. 154 ff.

[67] Mansi, XXII, 1038, Canon 1.

[68] Sess. XXIV, *De Reformatione Matrimonii*, Cap. I.

its publication. Its binding power was made contingent upon many conditions which were at times not fulfilled at all, at other times only doubtfully. It was binding only in parishes in which it was published and it took effect only thirty days after the publication. As a matter of fact, there were many parishes where it was never published due to the interference of secular rulers and even of ecclesiastical authorities themselves. In other parishes it was almost impossible to know whether or not it had been published. Again, even in communities where it had certainly been published its binding force might possibly become the object of doubt, especially in those parishes where there were many heretics. Beyond the place of publication, there were many other circumstances upon which the binding force of the new form depended so that doubts arose on all sides and the force of the decree was considerably weakened.[69] Since the decree could become binding through the force of custom another difficulty arose in the question of the validity of marriages.[70] Because of the great confusion which resulted from these circumstances, it cannot be doubted that many marriages were invalid due to neglect of the new form. Thus arose a new necessity and a new method in the convalidation of marriages—convalidating a marriage invalid because it lacked the proper form in the first celebration. This new regulation affected the marriages only of those persons who were bound by the Tridentine form. In regions where it was not in force the renewal of consent and the convalidation of marriage was effected in the same manner as before the Council of Trent.[71]

A marriage which was invalid because it lacked the prescribed form, could be convalidated only by a renewal of consent, and by the celebration of the marriage according to the form prescribed by the Council of Trent, i. e., before the parish priest and the witnesses. If the nullity were occult the renewal could take place secretly; but if the nullity were public the renewal had to take place publicly in order to repair any scandal occasioned by the invalid union. When the parties refused to contract anew according to the specified form there must be recourse in each case to the

[69] Wernz, *Jus Decretalium*, IV, nn. 158 ff.

[70] Benedict XIV, Ep. *Paucis Abhinc*, Mar. 19, 1758—*Fontes*, n. 447.

[71] Gasparri, *De Matrimonio* (3 Ed.), n. 1194.

3

Holy See for a correct solution of the difficulty.[72] The following case is an apparent exception. A marriage was invalidated because of failure to observe the form in a region where the form had been published and consequently was binding. The parties afterwards moved to a region in which the *Tametsi* decree had never been published and was not binding, and there established a domicile. Here of course clandestine marriages were valid. These two people could convalidate their marriage in this new domicile by renewing their consent either in words or by entering into the marriage relations with the proper marital intentions. It was not necessary that they observe the solemnities prescribed by the Council of Trent.[73]

Although the Council of Trent did not introduce new impediments strictly so-called it did affect the manner of convalidating marriages which were invalid because of impediments. This change had its origin in the new form, also. How were invalid marriages to be convalidated? What form was to be used? Must it always be public? The answer varied with the nature of the impediment. If the marriage had been null either because of the lack of consent or because of an impediment which had ceased it was necessary to renew the consent. If the invalidating defect was occult the renewal could be made privately either explicitly or implicitly; explicitly, that is, by a definite and external renewal of consent; implicitly, by a consent expressed by actions such as the performance of the conjugal duties or the free physical cohabitation with the proper marital intention. This implicit and explicit renewal of consent under the circumstances described was permitted if the Tridentine form had been observed in the first celebration of marriage.[74] But if the nullity of the previous marriage was public the renewal of consent had to be made according to the Tridentine form if the place wherein the renewal was made, was subject to that form; or if the parties concerned were bound by it.[75] But if the marriage

[72] S. C. S. Off., *Instr. Ad Archiep. Scopien.*, Nov. 15, 1882—*Coll.*, n. 1579.

[73] Wernz, *Jus Decretalium*, IV, 649, n. 7; Gasparri, *De Matrimonio* (Ed. 1900), n. 1146.

[74] Sanchez, *De Matrimonio*, II, Disp. 37, n. 3; Schmalzgrueber, IV, Part 1, Tit. 1, n. 415; Gasparri, *De Matrimonio* (3. ed.), n. 1407.

[75] S. R. R., Feb. 26, 1609—Pignatelli, *Consultationes Canonicae, VIII*, C. 27, nn. 4, 5; Benedict XI, V, *Institutiones Ecclesiasticae*, LXXXVII, n. LXII.

had formerly been celebrated according to the form of Trent, and later an occult impediment was discovered, the renewal could take place without repeating the form. It could be either express or tacit. This discipline obtained even in places where the decree *Tametsi* was in force, provided that in the first celebration of marriage the proper form had been observed.[76]

Another change noted after the Council of Trent had reference to dispensations from the impediment of affinity originating in sinful intercourse. Previous to the Council no clause requiring renewal of consent was found in the rescripts granting these dispensations, but after the Council the clause "de novo praestito consensu" was inserted. It was disputed whether or not the renewal should be public and finally it was decided that the renewal should be private if there was danger that scandal might arise from public renewal.[77]

The procedure for convalidating marriage nullified by impediment applies also to those that were null because of defect of consent. If both parties lacked proper consent both must renew it; if only one, it sufficed if he alone renewed it.[78] If the defect was external, consent had to be renewed in the presence of the pastor and two witnssses. But if the defect could not be proved in the external forum the party or parties were permitted to express their consent implicitly v. g., by the use of the marital right, provided they had already contracted in the prescribed form.[79] If the defect was such that it could be proved in the external forum the parties had to observe again the form of the Council of Trent in their act of convalidation.[80] Thus if a marriage was null because of a fear which was occult, nothing beyond the renewal of consent was prescribed if the Tridentine form had been observed in the

[76] Benedict XIV, *Institutiones Ecclesiasticae*, LXXXVII, n. LXII, LXIII; Gasparri, *De Matrimonio* (Ed. 1900), n. 1407; S. C. C. *Hispalen*, June 20, 1609—*Fontes*, n. 2378.

[77] "Circa Revalidationem Matrimoniorum Nulliter Initorum," *ASS*, II (1865), 52.

[78] Sanchez, *De Matrimonio*, II, Disp. 23, n. 11.

[79] Sanchez, *De Matrimonio*, IV, Disp. XVIII.

[80] S. C. C., Panorm, Sept. 30, 1719—*Thesaurus* I, 229; *Benedict* XIV, *Institutiones Ecclesticae*, LXXXVII, n. 62; Sanchez, *De Matrimonio*, II, Disp. XXXVII, n. 11. If they were not bound to observe the form they could even in this case renew consent privately.

first marriage. But if the impediment of fear could be proved in the external forum the renewal of consent had to be made publicly. In this latter case mere cohabitation or carnal intercourse was insufficient to effect convalidation. This discipline marks a change from the practice previous to the Council for at that time a marriage could be validated by mere cohabitation and carnal intercourse.[81]

It is necessary now to notice a difficulty which arose in connection with the renewal of consent. If the first marriage had been invalid because of an impediment, the second marriage could not be convalidated until both parties knew of the existence of the impediment.[82] This means that if one person was responsible for the impediment and the other had entered into the marriage in good faith, this second party would have to be told that his partner had known and concealed the impediment and the invalidity of the first marriage. It is not difficult to see what inconvenience and embarrassment this disclosure would sometimes cause. Nevertheless it was enjoined and a clause like this was added to the dispensations: "Dicta muliere (vel viro) de nullitate prioris consensus certiorata." Did the validity of the dispensation depend upon the fulfillment of this clause? It was a matter of dispute. Most canonists seem to think that the clause, since it was an ablative absolute, was essential and therefore necessary for the validity of the dispensation.[83] There was a strong insistence upon this same procedure when the marriage had taken place between pagans and Catholics, or between two converts. Such at least is the tenor of several responses of the Holy Office. An answer sent to the Vicar Apostolic of Su Tch Ansi, China, on January 12, 1769, instructed the missionaries that when marriage had been invalid because of disparity of worship, the consent must be renewed, but first the nullity of the former marriage must be made known to the infidel party.[84]

[81] Reiffenstuel, IV, Adnotatio LXVIII.

[82] Sanchez, *De Matrimonio*, VIII, Disp. 36, n. 3; Reiffenstuel, IV, Append. XIII, n. 587; St. Alphonsus, *Theologia Moralis*, V, n. 1115.

[83] Sanchez, *De Matrimonio*, VIII, Disp. 34, n. 61; Wernz, *Jus Decretalium*, IV, n. 651, note 10; Gasparri, *De Matrimonio* (3. ed.), nn. 1404, 1406; Benedict IV (*Institutiones Ecclesiasticae*, LXXXVII, n. 66 ff.) notes that this was the practice of the Sacred Penitentiary.

[84] *Coll.*, n. 472.

The evident difficulties which might arise from such disclosure of the impediment and the revelation of the fault or sin of the one who was its cause moved the German bishops at the Council of the Vatican to ask that such a clause be removed from the dispensations so that no doubt could arise about the validity of the new contract.[85] The result was that from 1885 this clause was modified to require that the informing should take place only when it can be done without grave danger.[86]

During the centuries intervening between the Council of Trent and the publication of the Code of Canon Law, there was no change in the legislation governing convalidation except that mentioned above, the mitigation in imposing the obligation of informing the party ignorant of the nullity. There was only one instruction of note on convalidation, that of Cardinal Caprara. He directed that marriages which were null because of an occult impediment must be convalidated by renewing consent in the presence of the parish priest and two witnesses but in a secret manner so that no scandal should arise from the convalidation. The fact of convalidation must be registered in the secret archives. If the impediment is public the renewal must take place publicly unless the local ordinary judges otherwise and permits it to be convalidated in the manner of the preceding marriage, but in this event all scandal must be removed.[87]

There is but one more slight change in the ordinary convalidation of marriage before the Code of Canon Law. It is contained in the decree *Ne Temere*.[88] It became effective on April 19, 1908. It obliged all Catholics of Latin rite to observe the prescribed form of marriage. Thus was secured a universal form of the marriage celebration.[89] Its effect on convalidation is more indirect than direct. If a marriage was contracted invalidly before the decree

[85] Martin, *Collectio Documentorum Omnium Concilii Vaticani*, p. 176.

[86] Wernz, *Jus Decretalium*, IV, n. 651, n. 10; Gasparri, *De Matrimonio* (3. ed.), n. 1406. Since the Code became effective no informing is required.

[87] *Instructio Cardinalis Caprara, Legati a Latere in Galliis, circa convalidationem Matrimoniorum Nulliter Initorum*—Zitelli, *De Dispensationibus Matrimonialibus*, Appendix VI, p. 175.

[88] S. C. C., Decretum "*Ne Temere*," Aug. 2, 1907—*Fontes*, n. 4340.

[89] Gasparri, *De Matrimonio* (Ed. 1932), n. 931; Wernz-Vidal, *Jus Canonicum*, V, n. 530; Cappello, *De Sacramentis*, III, n. 660.

Ne Temere became effective by persons who were subject to the decree *Tametsi* of the Council of Trent, the marriage must be renewed according to the *Ne Temere* form. If, on the other hand, they were not subject to the *Ne Temere* form at the time of convalidation they were not forced to renew consent according to that form. This is really an exception to the general rule contained in the *Ne Temere,* and not an innovation.[90]

One of the important developments of this period was the continued insistence upon renewal of consent. It is difficult to determine the exact date at which the renewal of consent became a requirement of ecclesiastical law. The early councils from the sixth to the tenth ecntury did not demand it when they granted special permission for those in invalid marriages to continue in them. Even in the tenth century when dispensations were granted to individuals to convalidate their marriage, there was no mention of renewal of consent in the rescripts.[91] The first demand for renewal is noticed in the thirteenth century.[92] It can scarcely be concluded from this isolated instance that the practice of demanding renewal of consent began exactly at that time; nor on the other hand that it was a universal requirement of the law. The matter is uncertain. It remains uncertain even to the time of the Council of Trent. Authors in general assert that there was no uniformity in the practice of demanding that consent be renewed before the Council of Trent.[93] For example, in dispensations that were granted before the Council from the impediment of affinity that arose from illicit *copula,* the clause demanding a renewal of consent was absent. This seems to have been the practice in granting dispensations from other occult impediments as well. Later the clause was inserted *de novo praestito consensu.*[94] There was no positive legislation on this matter in the Council of Trent. It seems therefore that insistence upon renewal of consent was the

[90] Lehmkuhl, *Theologia Moralis,* II, n. 524; Cronin, *The New Matrimonial Legislation,* p. 308.

[91] Rigantius, *Commentaria,* Reg. 49, nn. 6, 7.

[92] C. 7. X, *de eo qui duxit in matrimonium,* IV, 7.

[93] Scherer, *Handbuch des Kirchenrechts,* II, pp. 454, 500: Navarrus, IV, Consil. 14, De Sponsalibus, n. 1; D'Annibale, *Summula,* III, 365, note; Wernz, *Jus Decretalium,* IV, n. 610, note 20.

[94] Navarrus, *loc. cit.*

result of a gradual legal development which was given added impulse by the reforms of the Council. The uniformity in asking for renewal was due probably to the fact that the Church desired to reform radically the marriage law and safeguard the new form whose purpose might have been defeated if the parties could convalidate marriage without a renewal of consent. A marriage that was invalid because of an impediment that was occult could have been dissolved by the parties at any time on the ground of non-convalidation. Renewing consent insured and secured the validity in the eyes of the Church. Though it has been insisted on since, it was not made a formal law of the Church until the Code of Canon Law.

This last period of development brought the discipline of the convalidation of marriage almost to its completion. There is very little change in the legislation of the Code. After the Council of Trent there is scant legislation on the sacrament of matrimony with the exception of the decree *Ne Temere.* The changes that were noted were the results of particular interpretations of the decrees of the Council and the adaptation of its general decrees to particular situations. Of course it was to be expected that the applications for convalidation would increase during this period; the Church was growing rapidly and the number of marriages was increasing. All this, together with the growth of Protestantism and the weakening of the faith and the intermingling with those who had embraced heresy would naturally enough tend to produce an increase in invalid marriages, and the subsequent need of dispensations and convalidations. The result of all this was the development of the legislation on convalidation into its present complete stature in the Code of Canon Law.

CHAPTER III

RENEWAL OF CONSENT

The primary requirement for simple convalidation of marriage is the renewal of marital consent. It is, in fact, the very convalidation itself. In general, everything that is necessary for contracting marriage is necessary also for its convalidation because convalidation is in its essence a new marriage. But renewal of consent is so essential and so indispensable to simple convalidation that it merits special consideration. It marks, too, one of the chief differences between simple convalidation and the *sanatio in radice.* The latter, as has been noticed before, does not require a renewal of consent. On the contrary it always implies a dispensation from the renewal.[1] But the former, by a positive statement of law, always entails a new act of consent. This is true whether the marriage was invalid from an impediment or from defect of consent or lack of form.[2]

The manner of renewing consent varies with the circumstances of the invalidity. Whether it is to be public or private, internal or external, whether by one party or by both, will be discussed in the next chapter. The present chapter will treat only of the nature, the necessity, and the kinds of renewal.

ARTICLE I

The Nature of Renewal of Consent

Canon 1134 defines the act of renewal of consent as an " act of the will consenting to a marriage which is known to have been null from the beginning." From this it is seen that the renewal of consent is, in reality, a new consent,[3] a new act of the will distinct from and independent of the first act. It is separated from the first in time and in continuity and is entirely and thoroughly individual. The mind realizes the first consent was defective or at least ineffective, and now gives a new consent. It may have hap-

[1] Canon 1138.

[2] Canons 1133, § 62; 1135, 1136, 1137.

[3] Gasparri, *De Matrimonio* (Ed. 1932), 1186.

pened that in contracting the marriage no consent was given, or the consent may have been given, but ineffectively, because of an impediment or of failure to observe the canonical form. In either case the new consent given in the convalidation is called the renewal of consent.

It may be defined as an act of the will which here and now intends to contract a new marriage, to give and to receive at this moment the perpetual and exclusive rights peculiar to the marriage contract. An example will make the definition more clear. Two persons have contracted what they considered to be a valid marriage. They discover after a certain time that in reality their marriage is invalid because of a diriment impediment. In order now to convalidate it they must, after the removal of the impediment, make a new intention to marry and by a new act of the will give an entirely new consent.[4] Unless they make this new act the marriage will remain invalid. For according to Church Law there must be a new act of the will, directed to forming a new marriage with the knowledge that the former is invalid. But by means of the new act the invalid union is made a valid and true marriage and obtains all the effects of marriage both as sacrament and as contract.

The renewal is not, consequently, a mere continuance of the former consent nor a perseverance in it. It is not a renewal if two parties to a marriage should say "We renew now the consent we gave at the time we first contracted marriage." Nor is it an act which only confirms the former consent as if they added an oath to strengthen it. Neither is it a merely interpretative renewal, that is, an act or renewal of consent which would take place if the parties knew that it was necessary. For example, two persons are not aware that their union is invalid; but if they did know they would renew consent. Evidently in such a case there is no new act at all and hence it can not produce any effects.[5] It is also to be noted that the continued use of the marriage rights, or the prolonged cohabitation of the parties, is not in itself a renewal of consent. At most it is to be taken as a presumption of consent which cedes to proof of the contrary.[6]

[4] Payen, *De Matrimonio*, II, n. 2572, 1.

[5] Wernz-Vidal, *Jus Matrimoniale*, Vol. V, n. 457, note 13.

[6] *S. R. R. Dec.*, V (1913), Decis. XVI, in *Causa Neo-Eboracen*, Mar. 1, 1913, ad 21; Sanchez, *De Matrimonio*, IV, Disp. 18, n. 6.

In order that the renewal of consent be a new act of the will it is necessary that it be made with the knowledge that the former consent is invalid. This is deduced from the canon itself, which demands that the consent be given to a marriage "which it is evident was null from the beginning." It is intimated also in the following canons, 1133, § 1 and 1135, § 3, which state that the consent must be renewed by the one who is "consious of the impediment." The reason for this prescription of ecclesiastical law is found in the maxim—*nil volitum nisi praecognitum.* A person cannot give a valid consent to a new marriage unless he knows that he is contracting a new marriage and not merely confirming a former consent. And he cannot know that he is contracting a new marriage until he realizes that his former marriage is invalid. Unless he is aware that his marriage is invalid, the second consent is directed not to forming a new contract but to confirming a former union which is thought to be valid. That is all the person intends and his act cannot produce any effects beyond the intention, and hence cannot produce a new and valid marriage.[7]

If a person, for example, who erroneously considers himself to be validly married, renews his consent to that marriage and continues to live with his partner, exercising all the duties and the privileges of married life, he does not in any sense convalidate that marriage, as long as the error exists. He merely exercises his rights in view of the former consent.[8]

It may be debated whether or not a person, without the knowledge that the former union is invalid, can, absolutely speaking, give a consent which will be psychologically a new consent. Sanchez[9] denies that such a new consent is possible. Gasparri[10] and others[11] assert that it is possible even if one is convinced that the former consent is valid. This latter view seems to be correct. It is alto-

[7] Sanchez, *De Matrimonio,* II, Disp. XXXIV, n. 2; Disp. XXXVI, n. 6; Reiffenstuel, Lib. IV, Appen. n. 590; Schmalzgrueber, Lib. IV, Par. III, Tit. XVI, n. 263.

[8] Schmalzgrueber, Lib. IV, Par. I, Tit. I, n. 421.

[9] *De Matrimonio,* II, Disp. XXXIV, n. 2.

[10] *De Matrimonio* (3. ed.), n. 1307.

[11] St. Alphonsus, *Theologia Moralis,* VI, n. 1117; D'Annibale, *Summula Theologiae Moralis,* III, n. 483, note 17; Payen, *De Matrimonio,* II, n. 2554, § 3.

gether possible that a consent can be given if, as Gasparri says, two persons, believing that their marriage is valid, should intend and say "Let us contract marriage again"; or "I take you again as my wife, or as my husband."[12] But the Church has made it a positive law that there must be knowledge of the nullity of the former union before the renewal of consent can be effective. It will accept no other consent in simple convalidation.[13] If, therefore, two people are not aware that their marriage is invalid they cannot convalidate it unless in some manner the knowledge of that nullity is made known to them. The pastor therefore who realizes that a certain marriage in his parish in invalid, and that the partners to it are not aware of it, must inform them of the invalidity of their union, if he judges that they ought to convalidate it.

Thus the knowledge of the nullity is a strict requirement of ecclesiastical law. Once it has been established that the party or parties were not aware of the nullity of their marriage there is no possibility of proving its convalidation. This is evident from the practice of the Rota.[14] Because baptized non-Catholics also are bound by this law, it is easy to see that many of the invalid marriages of baptized non-Catholics will never be convalidated. It is not likely that they realize the invalidity of their marriage; it is difficult for them to know when a marriage in invalid, especially since they are subject to the impediments of Catholic ecclesiastical law, except when expressly exempt therefrom by the law itself.[15] They can scarcely be expected to know all the impediments which render marriage invalid. Nevertheless they must recognize the invalidity of their marriage before they can convalidate it. Their marriages, therefore, if invalid will usually remain so even though the parties live together peacefully and with the intention of living

[12] Gasparri, *l. c.*

[13] Chelodi, *Jus Matrimoniale*, n. 164.

[14] *In Causa Onasbrugen*, Jan. 11, 1912—*S. R. R. Decisiones*, IV (1912), Dec. III; *In Causa Nullitatis Matrimonii*, Dec. 21, 1912—*op. cit.*, Dec. XXXXI; *In Causa Neo-Eboracen.*, Mar. 1, 1913—V (1913), Dec. XVI; *In Causa Westmonasterien.*, Apr. 11, 1927—XIX (1927), Dec. XIV. There are many others to be found in the decisions of the Rota and in the decrees and instructions of the congregations of the Council and the Holy Office.

[15] Gasparri, *De Matrimonio* (Ed. 1932), n. 257.

as husband and wife.[16] It is highly probable, then, that the majority of invalid marriages of baptized non-Catholics are not convalidated.

Since the knowledge of the nullity of the first marriage is only of ecclesiastical law, it has no binding effect upon unbaptized non-Catholics. Hence if two unbaptized persons enter upon an invalid marriage they may convalidate it by continuing in their former consent after the impediment has ceased to exist.

It may be asked whether the knowledge of the exact cause of the nullity is required. For example: a pastor realizes that a certain marriage in his parish is null because at the time of the marriage the consent was vitiated by grave fear. The parties themselves are not aware of the nullity. If the pastor should choose to have the marriage convalidated, must he make known to the parties the cause of the nullity, or does it suffice merely to tell them that the marriage is null? It seems that a general knowledge of the nullity suffices. A person knowing that his marriage is null is capable of making a new act of consent which will be valid and distinct from the first act. The canon does not demand any more than the renewal of consent made with the knowledge that the marriage was invalid from the beginning.[17] It does not demand a more detailed knowledge or that the person be conscious of the specific cause of the nullity.[18] This opinion seems to be confirmed by a practice which existed under the former law. This case is this: if only one party knew that the marriage was invalid, he usually was required to inform the other party of the nullity before he could convalidate it.[19] He was not required to make known the exact cause of the nullity.[20] This is evident from the devices invented by the authors to reveal the nullity without revealing its cause.[21] For example, the party

[16] S. R. R., Jan. 11, 1912—*S. R. R. Dec.* IV (1912), Decis. III, *In Causa Onasbrugen*, ad 10; Dec. 21, 1912—IV (1912), Decis. XXXXI, *In Causa Nullitatis Matrimonii*, ad 7.

[17] Canon 1134.

[18] Payen, *De Matrimonio*, II, nn. 1715-1717.

[19] Benedict XIV, *Institutiones Ecclesiasticae*, LXXXVII, nn. LXXI-LXXVII.

[20] Reiffenstuel, IV, Append. XIII, n. 595.

[21] Sanchez, *De Matrimonio*, II, Disp. 36, n. 7; D'Annibale, *Summula Theologiae Moralis*, III, n. 485; Schmalzgrueber, IV, Par. III, Tit. XVI, n. 264.

conscious of the nullity might say to the other party: "When I married, I did not have true consent, let us renew it." This method was acknowledged effective and fulfilled all the conditions necessary for the convalidation.[22] Others also were suggested, but their effectiveness was the subject of controversy. In all cases though it is clear that the cause of the nullity need not be revealed. By analogy it may be concluded that under the Law of the Code, there is no necessity for telling the person or persons the exact reason why their marriage is null. Nothing beyond the knowledge of the nullity is required.

Article II

The Necessity of Renewing Consent

The new act of consent is essentially necessary to simple convalidation. The reason is that consent is essential to every marriage. It constitutes marriage in its being; it is the efficient cause which, when validly given by qualified persons, effects the contract and the sacrament of marriage.[23] But to produce these effects the consent must be valid both as a natural act of the will and as a juridic act, that is, in accord with the laws of the Church. If it does not fulfill the requirements of both these demands it is incapable of constituting a marriage. Thus a person who gives a consent under the influence of insanity, has not a naturally valid consent and therefore there is no marriage. Natural law invalidates this act. Even a naturally valid act can be ineffective if it does not comply with the law of the Church. Two Catholics who are bound by the canonical form of marriage must exchange their consent in the presence of the pastor and two witnesses. If they neglect to observe this form, their consent is ineffective. Juridically viewed it does not exist. Since it does not exist it must be supplied, otherwise the marriage cannot be convalidated, for without consent there is no marriage. In this case it can be supplied only by the parties themselves.

The canons leave no doubt about the necessity of renewing con-

[22] Gasparri, *De Matrimonio* (3. ed.), n. 1405; Reiffenstuel, V, Append. XIII, nn. 596-604; Benedict XIV, *Institutiones Ecclesiasticae*, Inst. LXXXVII, nn. LXXI-LXXXIX.

[23] Canon 1081; c. 25, X, *De sponsalibus et matrimonio*, IV, 1.

sent. Canon 1133, § 2, prescribes that "this renewal of consent is required by ecclesiastical law for validity even if both parties gave their consent in the beginning and did not afterwards recall it." The necessity is evident; the canon demands a renewal of consent even when the first consent was a naturally valid act, but has been ineffective juridically. More than that, it requires a renewal even if that naturally valid consent still perseveres in the will of the persons who first gave it.

In this law the Code introduces a new statute into the common law of the Church. Until the Code was promulgated there was no general law of the Church demanding that consent be renewed.[24] Though not a part of the common law in practice the renewal of consent was very often demanded by the rescripts which granted dispensations to convalidate marriages. The practice seems to have originated in the Decretals of Gregory IX, in which a renewal was demanded of a person who had contracted an invalid marriage through error.[25] Up to the time of the Council of Trent there was no uniform practice of demanding a new consent, although from the twelfth century onward there was an increase in the practice and it assumed a certain uniformity at the time of the Council.[26] Since the Council of Trent that practice became quite uniform, though it was made a formal law only in the Code.[27]

The law of the Code demands that consent must always be renewed, at least by the party who is conscious of the invalidity of the marriage. It matters not what the source of the invalidity is, whether it be a diriment impediment, or lack of form, or defect of consent; it can be corrected only by a renewal of consent.[28]

[24] Gasparri, *De Matrimonio* (Ed. 1932), n. 1191; Benedict XIV, *Institutiones Ecclesiasticae*, LXXXVII, n. LXVIII.

[25] C. 2, 4, X, *de conjugio servorum*, IV, 9; Gasparri, *De Matrimonio* (Ed. 1932), n. 1191.

[26] Wernz, *Jus Decretalium*, IV, n. 610, note 20; Navarrus, Lib. IV, Consil. 14, *De Sponsalibus*, n. 1; Gasparri, *De Matrimonio* (3. ed.), n. 1395.

[27] Cf. Chapter II, Article 3, for history of this institute.

[28] Canons 1133, § 1; 1136, § 1; 1137. If the marriage is invalid because of lack of consent, or from defective consent, it is perhaps more correct to say that the consent in the convalidation is "given" rather than "renewed," because it never actually existed before. But authors generally use the term "renew" in this connection, and it shall be used here.

Thus after an invalid marriage, until the proper renewal of consent is made, either of the parties is free to leave and to contract another marriage which will be valid. The necessity of this new act of consent is absolute; there is no excuse or exception. It may happen that the parties are unaware of the invalidity of their marriage and therefore do not even suspect that they must renew consent; it may be that they are aware of the invalidity but do not realize that they have to renew their consent; it may happen that the one party or both are unable to give that new act of consent, because, for example, they have become insane; finally, one or both parties may refuse to renew consent; in all these cases the marriage remains invalid. For just as in the beginning no human power could supply for their lack of consent, so now, in simple convalidation no human power can supply for their failure to renew consent. Such situations can be saved only by obtaining a *sanatio in radice,* if the original consent of both parties still exists.

Is this renewal of consent required by natural law? In only one case does natural law require renewal of consent in convalidation, when the marriage has been invalid because consent was entirely lacking in the first celebration. By its very nature marriage is a contract between two persons and is constituted in its being by their consent. If one (or both) omits to give his consent the contract is not completed and it is invalid by natural law. It will continue to be invalid as long as consent is withheld by the party who formerly did not consent because no other human power can supply the missing consent. In this case then natural law requires a renewal of consent as an essential condition for convalidation.

But if a naturally valid consent which had been given in the first celebration of marriage was rendered ineffective by an impediment or by failure to observe the prescribed form, does the necessity of renewing this consent come from natural or merely ecclesiastical law? Previous to the Code canonists were divided in their teaching. There was, as has been remarked before, no general ecclesiastical law which imposed renewal of consent and in its absence authors, while they admitted the obligation of renewal, differed on the question of its source. Those canonists [29] who maintained that renewal of consent

[29] Sanchez, *De Matrimonio,* II, Disp. XXXV, n. 2; Reiffenstuel, Lib. IV, Append. n. 585; Schmalzgrueber, Lib. IV, Tit. XVI, nn. 257 ff.; Pontius, Lib. IV, Cap. XXXIV, n. 3.

was a necessity imposed by natural law argued that the first consent was naturally invalid and therefore did not exist. The reason is based on the fact that the act of consent was concerned with and directed to an object which was not proper matter for a matrimonial consent and therefore could not serve as the basis for that consent. Because it lacked this essential basis the consent itself was entirely vitiated and consequently must be regarded as non-existent. Since it did not exist from the very beginning, it follows that it could not persevere in existence and therefore could never be capable of effecting a valid marriage. Consequently it was necessary by natural law—which always demands consent for a valid marriage—that consent be renewed for an effective convalidation.

Other canonists [30] insisted the necessity of renewal of consent was imposed by ecclesiastical law only. Renewal of consent, they assert, would be necessary by natural law only if the consent first given was invalid or did not persevere at the time of the convalidation. But in the case under consideration (when the consent was rendered ineffective by an impediment or neglect of form) the consent was not invalid and the supposition is that it persevered at the time of convalidation. There is no need therefore of renewing it unless a renewal were prescribed by ecclesiastical law. That the consent which was first given was valid seems to be proved from the following arguments. The act of consent in itself belongs entirely to the will; it depends for its existence and its natural validity upon the will alone; external circumstances do not affect the act in itself. When therefore a person elicits an act of consent in view of a matrimonial contract that act exists in the will as true act of consent with its own physical existence. Whether or not it will effect the purposes of the person consenting matters not. Once the will acts the consent is given before all reference to external circumstances, precisely because it is an act of the will and is not determined nor limited by the material to which it is directed. The person who is the cause of the consent may revoke it by a later act, he may prevent the perseverance of the consent, and counteract its effects by a

[30] Wernz, *Jus Decretalium*, IV, 648-50; Gasparri, *De Matrimonio* (3. ed.), n. 1395; Lehmkuhl, *Theologia Moralis*, II, n. 1053; De Becker, *De Sponsalibus et Matrimonio* (ed. 1896), p. 338; Konings, *Theologia Moralis* (ed. 7), I, n. 1634, II; Gury, *Compendium Theologiae Moralis* (Ed. 1869), II, 896.

distinct and contrary act of his will, but his former consent has already actually existed and has been naturally valid and real. Hence the act of consent can be a naturally valid act of the will of the person even in the presence of an impediment, which is a merely external circumstance that prevents the act of the will from having its effect. It is in their failure to distinguish between the act itself in the will and the production of its external effects that the proponents of "renewal by natural law" err. Even if the will does give a valid act of consent the effects which that act is calculated to produce may be limited or obstructed altogether by a circumstance which does not touch the act itself. Thus the consent may be limited externally with regard to the canonical and juridical effects it would ordinarily produce. Ecclesiastical law need not always and under all circumstances permit the valid internal consent of persons to produce its intended effects, but by instituting impediments it may curtail the natural aptness of the act. But in no sense does it invalidate the act itself. That remains valid. The fact that the juridic effect, the contracting of marriage, is not realized is due solely to an external circumstance, which cannot exert any vitiating influence on an entirely internal act. Not the act, but the improper matter to which it is directed is responsible for the invalidity. Since the consent was valid in the beginning, it will continue to be valid until revoked by the party who gave it. If it does persevere it will take its effect as soon as the external obstacles are removed. Hence there is no necessity for renewal unless ecclesiastical law prescribes it.

This latter opinion has been confirmed by the practice of the Church in granting a *sanatio in radice.* As explained before the *sanatio* is granted to convalidate invalid marriages when the parties refuse or are not able to renew consent. If the first consent has been naturally valid and is still persevering, the Church under certain circumstances grants a dispensation from the renewal of consent in the form of a *sanatio.* The *sanatio* at the same time removes all obstacles which prevented the consent from producing its canonical effects. The result of the *sanatio* is the convalidation of marriage. Such a practice cannot be explained except by concluding that the Church considers the first consent a naturally valid act and capable in itself of producing a valid marriage. If the consent had not been valid it would be necessary now by natural law to renew it under pain of not contracting marriage for no power on earth can dispense those things which are necessary by natural law. Since the Church does claim and exercise the power of granting such dispensations, it acknowledges that the law from which it dispenses has the Church as its source, for dispensations can be granted only by the authority which made the law. This practice of the Church supports the contention that consent, validly given and not recalled, must be renewed to convalidate marriage only because ecclesiastical law demands a renewal.

It might be objected that, even conceding the possibility of a valid consent in the case where the impediment is not known or adverted to, consent cannot be possible if the impediment is known, for a person who has knowledge that his act is going to be ineffective cannot make a valid act. The mind here is concerned with the impossible. It is conceded that the mind does dwell upon the fact that no marriage is possible because of the impediment. But consent is an act of the will, not of the mind, and therefore the former faculty can form an act of consent to marriage, i. e., to the mutual exchange of rights between man and woman. This may happen in various ways: the person may move his will to act "because he may for some reason excuse himself from the impediment, or because he thinks that later the whole affair will be rectified, or he may even act directly against the law." [31] In these cases there may be true matrimonial consent. It is interesting to note that even those who maintain that necessity of renewal comes from natural law admit that the consent may be valid if the impediment is merely putative.[32] It is difficult to understand how they can distinguish between a real and a putative impediment in this regard for at the time the consent is given both have the same effect upon the act of the will for they both have real existence in the mind of the person who consents. It must be concluded that they place the validity of consent not in the act of the will but in the impediment itself. In that event their argument loses all its conviction for consent is and always must be an internal act of the will. The controversy has been settled by the Code in Canon 1133, § 2, in

[31] Gasparri, *De Matrimonio* (Ed. 1932), n. 812.
[32] Sanchez, *De Matrimonio*, II, Disp. XXXV, nn. 1, 2.

which canon it has put its stamp of approval upon the opinion that asserts the renewal is necessary not by natural, but only by ecclesiastical, law.[33]

This question assumes practical importance because of its relation to the convalidation of marriages contracted by unbaptized persons. Since they are not bound by purely ecclesiastical law, because they are not subjects of the Church, it is not necessary for them to renew their consent in convalidating their marriage.[34] It is sufficient if the consent exchanged by the parties on the occasion of the first ceremony still perseveres. Perseverance, not renewal, is required and is sufficient for convalidation of the marriages of unbaptized persons. The former consent in itself was valid and would have effected a valid marriage but for the presence of an impediment which prevented the naturally valid consent from producing its intended results—a valid marriage. But the impediment did not destroy the validity of the consent nor in any manner injure the act in itself and therefore the consent (if it perseveres) still has within itself the power to effect a valid marriage whenever the external obstacle are removed. The impediment, as it were, holds the efficacy of the consent in check so that it cannot produce its proper effect upon the matter to which it is directed. When the check is removed there is nothing further to restrain the consent and it reaches out to its object and the resulting union is a valid marriage. This follows from the very notion of marriage itself as a contract which is constituted by the consent of two persons qualified by law to give consent. By the removal of the impediment the persons previously disqualified are now made capable of marriage and as their consent still endures there is nothing lacking now from the contract and therefore it is effected. The moment the impediment is removed in that moment the marriage is convalidated without any other formality of the parties. It matters not whether the two persons are aware of the convalidation, as long as the consent is present in both, for it is the union of their mutual and valid consent and nothing else that constitutes marriage. No supple-

[33] Gasparri, *De Matrimonio* (Ed. 1932), nn. 1190, 1191; Wernz-Vidal, *Jus Canonicum,* IV, n. 656; Payen, *De Matrimonio,* II, nn. 2555, 2572; Cappello, *De Sacramentis,* III, n. 844, 4º.

[34] Canon 12; Maroto, *Institutiones Juris Canonici,* I, n. 196.

mentary act of the parties is required, neither a formality of renewal, nor a confirmation of the former consent. Hence in the case of two unbaptized persons there is no need for any act of wilful cohabitation or the use of the marriage right *animo maritali* or any other act to make the contract binding. These acts constitute valuable proof attesting to the perseverance of the former consent, or they can be used as external manifestations of the perseverance. But they are not necessary for the convalidation; before these and all other acts the marriage is validated by the mere perseverance in consent. Perseverance in a formerly given valid consent is alone necessary and alone sufficient for convalidation of invalid marriages of unbaptized persons.

These principles become more clear in the following example. Two unbaptized persons have contracted a marriage which is invalid because of the impediment of *ligamen,* which is an impediment of natural law and therefore invalidates all marriages. As long as the impediment exists their marriage will remain invalid because the consent given cannot produce its effect. But if the impediment is removed, for example by the death of the first husband or wife and if the consent given at the time of the second marriage still endures in the two parties to the second marriage, the latter union is validated at the very moment in which the impediment is removed. There is no need for the parties to renew their consent, nor even to realize that the impediment formerly existing has been removed. Their marriage becomes valid without any formality upon the removal of the impediment. But under like circumstances two Catholics would be under the strict obligation to renew consent after the impediment has been removed and they must also have been aware that the former marriage was invalid.

It is important to have this distinction in mind when there is question of the marriage of unbaptized persons. The rapid growth of divorce [35] has increased the number of invalid marriages due to the impediment of *ligamen* which leaves null and void the attempted marriages of unbaptized as well as of baptized persons. In view of this it would seem that most of the marriages contracted after divorce are invalid because of the prior marriage. But it is

[35] Cf. *Marriage and Divorce* (Government Printing Office, Washington, D. C., 1928); Dept. of Commerce.

necessary carefully to investigate the circumstances in each case to discover with certainty whether or not the second marriage has been convalidated. If the former partner, who has been divorced, has died, the second marriage is often validated because the impediment has been removed and the consent given to the second marriage still endures.[36] The following is an interesting case and indicates the many possibilities for convalidation existing in the marriages of those not baptized. Two unbaptized persons are validly married. The husband divorces his wife and marries a second unbaptized woman. The second marriage is evidently invalid because of the actual existence of the first. In the meantime his first wife becomes a Catholic, is baptized, and breaks the bond of the first marriage by the use of the Pauline privilege.[37] Thus the impediment of *ligamen* is removed. By that very fact the second marriage of her former husband is convalidated, provided, of course, that he and his present partner retain their marital consent. The reason is that upon the removal of the impediment the consent obtains its effects immediately, since the parties not being baptized are not bound to renew consent. Such a convalidated marriage is recognized by the Church as valid. If therefore these two parties are afterwards converted to the Catholic Church, they need not renew consent, not even for the sake of greater certainty. The marriage has already been convalidated and remains so.[38]

The necessity of renewing consent will not present itself in all cases of convalidation. If both parties are baptized they are bound by the law of the Church,[39] and must renew consent. If both parties are not baptized the consent need not be renewed because renewal is required only by Church law which has no binding force on the unbaptized in this instance. If the marriage has been contracted between a baptized and an unbaptized person both more probably must renew their consent, the former because he is directly bound by ecclesiastical law, and the latter because, by reason of

[36] This example must not be confused with the case of Canon 1139, § 2, where it is stated that the Church does not grant a *sanatio* for marriages contracted invalidly because of an impediment of divine law.

[37] Canon 1126.

[38] Payen, *De Matrimonio*, II, 2578, § 1.

[39] Canon 87; Maroto, *Institutiones Juris Canonici*, I, n. 196.

his marriage to a baptized person, he becomes indirectly subject to it.[40] If the one party is certainly not baptized and the other only doubtfully so neither is bound to renew consent; the former because he is certainly not bound by ecclesiastical law and the latter because she is not bound by a doubtful law. *Lex dubia non obligat.*[41] This opinion is not incontestably certain.[42] but it forms the basis for a practical procedure especially if it is foreseen that the parties, or one of them, will not renew consent. Since in practice this case will come to the attention of the pastor only after the conversion of one of the parties, and since they will then be under the necessity of renewing consent according to the canonical form, it may frequently happen that the still unconverted party will refuse to renew consent before the priest. In this case he should not be required to do so.[43]

Article III

Kinds of Renewal of Consent

Although consent must be renewed, the renewal need not always be manifested in the same way. The canons which regulate the renewal use such terms as *private* renewal; [44] *external,*[45] and *internal* [46] and *renewal in the form prescribed by law.*[47]

It is important to understand each of these terms because at times the validity of the convalidation will depend upon the correct use of them. Thus, for example, if parties are directed to renew consent in the form prescribed by law the convalidation would be invalid if it were to take place privately.

Private renewal is that which is made without the presence of the pastor and of the witnesses prescribed by law for the canonical form of marriage.[48] It usually is given in the presence of the

[40] Payen, *De Matrimonio,* II, 2572; Cappello, *De Sacramentis,* III, n. 67.

[41] Canon 15; Gasparri, *De Matrimonio* (Ed. 1932), n. 1193; A Coronata, *Institutiones Juris Canonici,* I, n. 14, 3; Vermeersch-Creusen, *Epitome,* I, n. 106, § 3.

[42] Cf. Arendt, "Brevis Animadversio"—*Jus Pontificium,* V (1925), 135, *secundum assertum.*

[43] Schaaf, "Is Convalidation of a Convert's Marriage Necessary?"—*AER,* XCV (1936), 91.

[44] Canon 1135, § 2.

[45] Canon 1136, § 3.

[46] Canon 1136, § 2.

[47] Canon 1136, § 3.

[48] Canons 1094-1099.

parties only, or even without the second party, if only one renews consent. This private renewal becomes secret when it is made in such a manner that others do not know about it.[49] The two terms, "private" and "secret," are not identical. "Private" has reference more to the possibility of proof; "secret," to the knowledge that others may have of it. Thus a secret renewal of consent is of necessity a private renewal because it cannot be proved in the external forum; but a private renewal is not always secret, because even if not made in the public forum it may have come to the knowledge of others.[50]

Opposed to private renewal is the renewal that is made according to the form prescribed by law. Usually it is called public renewal, because it furnishes legal proof in the external forum that the marriage has been convalidated. It requires the presence of the pastor and two witnesses;[51] unless in an extraordinary case, the parties are not bound to observe the form of marriage or they are exempt from it. Thus, for example, two baptized non-Catholics could publicly renew their consent without the presence of a priest and the two witnesses, because they are expressly exempt from the observance of the form.[52]

The internal renewal of consent remains entirely within the will of the person who makes it. There is no outward manifestation of it. Once it is manifested externally by word or action it becomes an external renewal. One must not identify this external renewal with that which is public. The latter includes always the observance of the substantial form of marriage; the former imports nothing more than an outward manifestation of the act of the will. A public renewal therefore must necessarily be external, but an external renewal is not necessarily public.

The terms become clearer by examples. If two parties to an invalid marriage renew consent in the presence of the pastor and two witnesses, the renewal is public; if they renew it merely in

[49] This secret renewal must be distinguished from the secrecy demanded in "marriages of conscience." In the latter situation the canonical form of marriage is observed. Cf. Canons 1104-1107.

[50] Payen, *De Matrimonio*, II, n. 2558; Gasparri, *De Matrimonio* (Ed. 1932), n. 1199; Cappello, *De Sacramentis*, III, n. 845, 2.

[51] Canons 1094-1099.

[52] Canon 1099, § 2.

the presence of each other, the renewal is private. But in both of these instances the renewal is external because it is manifested outwardly. If one of the parties renews his consent by an act that is kept entirely within his own will, and which is in no manner externally manifested, the renewal is internal. In this case it is secret also because no one except the one renewing consent has knowledge of it.

CHAPTER IV

CONVALIDATION FOLLOWING A DIRIMENT IMPEDIMENT

Canon 1133, § 1. Ad convalidandum matrimonium irritum ob impedimentum dirimens, requiritur ut cesset vel dispensetur impedimentum et consensum renovet saltem pars impedimenti conscia.

An analysis of this canon discloses the conditions that must be fulfilled in convalidating a marriage that has been invalid because of a diriment impediment. First, it is necessary that the impediment must be removed, and second, the consent must be renewed. It may be noted that the impediment mentioned must be a diriment impediment, for merely prohibitive impediments do not invalidate a marriage.[1] It does not matter whether the impediment exists only in the one party, or in both; in both cases it invalidates the marriage and must be removed.[2] The canon suggests two way in which the impediments may be removed, either by cessation of the impediment without dispensation (*cesset*), or by a dispensation given by a competent superior (*dispensetur*).

Article I

The Removal of the Impediment

The canon presupposes that the impediment can be removed. If removal is impossible there can be no convalidation for the renewal of consent will be as ineffective as was the first act of consent. Hence marriages that are invalid because of impediments of divine (both natural and positive) law, can never be validated.[3] These impediments are blood relationship of the first degree, between father and daughter or mother and son;[4] impotency that cannot

[1] Canon 1036.

[2] Canon 1036, § 3.

[3] Sanchez, *De Matrimonio*, VIII, Disp. VI, n. 10.

[4] Sanchez, *De Matrimonio*, VII, Disp. LI, n. 7; St. Thomas, In IV, Dist. 41, qu. un., art. 1.

be remedied, and *ligamen,* which results from a consummated valid marriage which still exists. In cases in which these impediments occur the marriage cannot be validated. Even in certain impediments of ecclesiastical law to be mentioned below convalidation is practically impossible because the Church refuses to grant dispensations from them.

If the impediment can be removed the process of convalidation is governed by the canon quoted. Some impediments can be removed only by a dispensation, others may disappear of their own nature when there is a change of circumstances. Thus the impediment of age vanishes with the passing of time when the proper age has been reached. Others may disappear by a change of will in the persons concerned. Thus disparity of worship ceases when the unbaptized party is converted and baptized; *ligamen* ceases when the marriage bond upon which it depends is broken; abduction ceases when the abductor places the girl abducted in a place where she is free from his domination and secure against duress. Finally, a change of law may also cause the cessation of impediments, as happened when the Code of Canon law became effective.

Other impediments because of their nature are perpetual and can be removed only by dispensation granted by competent superiors. These are sacred orders, solemn vows, crime, consanguinity, affinity, public propriety, spiritual and legal relationship. All these may be dispensed by the supreme power of the Church. But it must be remembered that the Church does not dispense in all these cases, even though she has the power to do so. Dispensations usually are not granted if there is any doubt whether the impediment is of the natural law, as consanguinity between brother and sister.[5] So also, dispensations from the impediment of sacred orders if they involve the episcopacy, or from the impediment of crime which involves murder, are not granted. The latter is dispensed at times in danger of death or in occult cases in the internal forum.[6] As regards dispensations from the other impediments, it is to be noted that dispensations from the priesthood, from affinity in the direct line and from abduction are obtained only with difficulty. In all other cases dispensations may be obtained. In applying for and in

[5] Cappello, *De Sacramentis,* III, n. 224, § 2.

[6] Cappello, *De Sacramentis,* III, n. 224.

granting them the canons which govern dispensations must be observed.[7]

In asking for the dispensation no other cause need be stated than the convalidation of the marriage. This is considered a grave and sufficient cause.[8] Very often it is not the only cause, usually there is also the necessity of legitimizing the children born of the invalid union or of terminating public or private concubinage. Convalidation is considered a grave cause for the reason that it is necessary to repair the scandal and to correct the evils that already have resulted from the invalid union. If the nullity of the marriage is not known, the parties cannot be separated without scandal to the public. If the nullity is known, the scandal can be repaired most effectively by convalidating the marriage. Very often the private good of the parties themselves, for example, the avoidance of the occasion of sin when they cannot separate, will constitute a reason for asking the dispensation.

Formerly, to obtain a dispensation the marriage had to be contracted in good faith and in the form prescribed by law.[9] By contracting an invalid union in bad faith the parties lost their right to ask for a dispensation. Even in this case convalidation could be adduced as a cause but owing to the bad faith of the parties the dispensation was obtained only with difficulty and sometimes denied altogether.[10] At present bad faith does not have the same effect.[11] Nor is it required now that the marriage should have been contracted in the form prescribed by law.[12]

In the petition for a dispensation to convalidate marriage it is necessary to mention not only the cause but also the circumstances that accompany it. The difficulty or the ease with which the dispensation is granted depends upon these circumstances, which often

[7] Cf. Canons 80-86; 1043-1057.

[8] Sanchez, *De Matrimonio*, VIII, Disp. XIX, n. 33; Gasparri, *De Matrimonio* (Ed. 1904), n. 365.

[9] Council of Trent, Sess. XXIV, *De Reformatione Matrimonii.*, Cap. V; S. C. Prop. Fid., Instr., May 9, 1877, n. 6—*Coll.*, n. 1470; De Becker, *De Matrimonio*, p. 322.

[10] De Smet, *Betrothment and Marriage*, II, n. 824.

[11] S. C. S. Off. *Leopolien.* Mar. 18, 1891—*Coll.*, n. 1749; Chelodi, *Jus Matrimoniale*, n. 46; Wernz, *Jus Decretalium*, IV, n. 630, note 158; Zitelli, *De Dispensationibus Matrimonialibus*, p. 65.

[12] Payen, *De Matimonio*, I, n. 750.

reveal the attitude of the parties toward the law. It should be stated whether the marriage was contracted in good faith, or bad, whether the parties were aware of the impediment, and whether the banns were published and the form observed.[13] It is not required to state, at least not for the validity of the dispensation, that the parties attempted marriage with the intention of obtaining a dispensation more easily.[14] Nor is it necessary, certainly not for validity, to mention that the invalid union was consummated with the same purpose in view.[15] Formerly it had been necessary to mention the fact of consummation, but at the request of a number of bishops the Holy Office ceased to insist upon it.[16]

If the invalid union results from an attempted civil marriage, there is no need to express anything but that fact in the petition. It suffices of itself as a cause for granting the dispensation. In this case it is not necessary to make known the intention which the parties had in entering upon a civil union.[17]

As noted above, certain impediments ceased to bind because they were abrogated by the Code of Canon Law, May 19, 1918. What is to be said of marriages that were contracted invalidly before that time because of one of these impediments? For example, if two persons, who were related in the fourth degree of consanguinity married before the Code, their marriage was invalid.[18] But since the Code became effective that degree of consanguinity is not a diriment impediment to marriage. Was the invalid marriage of these relatives convalidated by the mere fact that the impediment to their marriage ceased to exist? The answer, given by the Pontifical Commission for the Authentic Interpretation of the Code,[19]

[13] Gasparri, *De Matrimonio* (Ed. 1932), n. 342; Cappello, *De Sacramentis,* III, n. 275, 7°; S. C. Prop. Fid., Instr., May 9, 1877—*Coll.*, 1470, n. 6.

[14] Wernz, *Jus Decretalium,* IV, n. 636, note 179; Gasparri, *De Matrimonio* (Ed. 1932), 342, note 2; Payen, *De Matrimonio,* I, n. 785.

[15] Gasparri, *De Matrimonio* (Ed. 1932), n. 342, note 2; Payen, *De Matrimonio,* I, n. 785, 2; Cappello, *De Sacramentis,* III, n. 275, 7°.

[16] S. C. S. Off., *Leopolien.*, Mar. 18, 1891—*Coll.*, 1749; *Encyc. Litt.*, June 25, 1885—*Coll.*, 1635.

[17] Payen, *De Matrimonio,* I, n. 785, 3.

[18] Lateran Council (1215), Cap. L—Mansi, XXII; Sanchez, *De Matrimonio,* VII, Disp. LIII, n. 1; Gasparri, *De Matrimonio* (3 ed.), n. 767.

[19] June 3, 1918, n. 7—*AAS,* X (1918), 346.

is that the marriage was not convalidated by the mere abrogation of the impediment; the consent must be renewed. Although the marriage was contracted under the old canon law its convalidation is regulated by the law now in force. It is not, of course, necessary to ask for a dispensation, since the impediment no longer exists.[20] But the parties must know that their marriage is invalid, and with that knowledge renew their consent.

It is evident that all diriment impediments, if more than one are present, must be removed. In the event that a second impediment arises after the first has been removed, a dispensation must be obtained—if that is possible—from this second impediment before the consent can be effectively renewed. If this second impediment is one of natural law the marriage cannot be convalidated even though the impediment which first rendered the marriage invalid has lapsed either by cessation (of its nature) or by dispensation.

Article II

The Renewal of Consent

The removal of the impediment qualifies the parties to give a new and effective matrimonial consent. The manner in which they renew their consent is determined in each case by the nature of the impediment which caused the nullity of their first union. The canons distinguish between public and occult impediments, and, in the event the impediment is occult, between those known to one and those known to both parties.

Section I

After a Public Impediment

Canon 1135, § 1. Si impedimentum sit publicum, consensus ab utraque parte renovandus est forma jure praescripta.

An impediment is public when it can be proved in the external forum.[21] Its publicity may be determined in two ways: either the fact upon which it depends is known to the public (*de facto*),

[20] *Periodica*, IX (1921), 154, n. 7.

[21] Canon 1037.

or by its nature (*natura sua*) it is capable of being proved publicly, although the knowledge of the fact upon which it depends is not yet public. The impediment of age is public because by its nature, it can be proved, for example, from the baptismal registers even though the fact of the actual age be hidden. But if the age of the person about to marry is known to at least two persons who can prove it then the impediment of age is public by fact as well as by nature. The impediment of crime, which usually depends in part upon a hidden fact, can become a public impediment if the circumstances come to the knowledge of those who can prove it in public.

The word " public " in this canon includes all public impediments whether they are public by nature or in fact. Since both classes of impediments can be proved in the external forum they beget an invalidity which is public and therefore they both fall within the limits of this canon.[22] Does the canon include also those impediments which are sometimes called materially public and formally occult, that is, when the fact, which is the source of the impediment, is known, but it is not recognized that this fact is the cause of an impediment? For example, it is known that a certain man and woman have murdered the latter's husband but it is not known that from such a murder the impediment of crime arises. All such impediments are included in the canon because the fact which is their source is public and can at any time be proved in the external forum. Marriages invalid from this impediment must be convalidated according to the directions in this canon.[23] In the above case, suppose that the fact of the homicide is known, but it is mistaken for an accident and not for the wilful murder it really is. Would the case then come under the class of public impediments? It seems not. The fact is indeed known but it is not known in its entirety, nor can it be proved in the external forum to be an impediment. The presence of the conditions necessary for incurring the impediment cannot be proved since the death is thought to be the result of an accident. It is considered an occult rather than a public impediment.[24]

[22] Chelodi, *Jus Matrimoniale*, n. 164.

[23] Cf. Pontifical Commission for the Authentic Interpretation of the Code, June 25, 1932—*AAS*, XXIV (1932), 284.

[24] Cappello, *De Sacramentis*, III, n. 200.

In all cases of public impediments, the consent must be renewed in the form prescribed by law. That form requires ordinarily the presence of the pastor or another duly authorized priest and two witnesses.[25] The reason for the use of the form is to insure a renewal of consent that is public. The impediment was public as also was the nullity of the marriage so that in the external forum there was no marriage at all. To avoid scandal that may result from such a situation, as well as to protect the children from the stigma of illegitimacy, it must be evident in the external forum that the marriage has been made valid.[26] This is best secured by the use of the public form.

Although a public renewal of consent is necessary for the validity of the convalidation, it may happen that it can be made in a manner that is partially secret, that is without the presence of any persons except those who are required for the canonical form.[27] It has the publicity required by law, but it is not public in the sense that the knowledge of the convalidation is divulged to others. If, for example, a marriage is invalid because of an impediment which is public by nature but not in fact the renewal of consent in this quasi-secret manner is warranted by the fact that an altogether public renewal might be a source of scandal to the public and of embarrassment to the parties. To avoid both, the consent might be exchanged even in a private home. For this the permission of the Ordinary is necessary. He may also grant permission for this quasi-secret renewal even when the impediment is publicly known. In this event the witnesses should be instructed to divulge discreetly the fact that the marriage has been convalidated in order to avoid scandal of those who are aware the impediment existed.[28]

If the parties are exempt from the observance of the form in the celebration of marriage they are exempt from it also in convalidation. This affects particularly baptized non-Catholics. Although

[25] Cf. Canons 1094-1099.

[26] Schmalzgrueber, IV, Tit. XVI, n. 276.

[27] This convalidation must not be identified with the marriage of conscience (Canons 1104-1107) though it is similar to it.

[28] Instructio Cardinalis Caprara . . . circa Revalidationem Matrimoniorum Nulliter Initorum, n. 7—Zitelli, *De Dispensationibus Matrimonialibus*, Append. VI; Gasparri, *De Matrimonio* (Ed. 1904), n. 1400; Cappello, *De Sacramentis*, III, n. 845; Payen, *De Matrimonio*, II, n. 2557.

they are bound in general by the laws of convalidation, they are exempt from the observance of the form.[29] So also are those children of non-Catholic parents who have been baptized in the Catholic Church, but who have been educated from childhood, that is, from their seventh year, in a heretical or schismatical sect or if educated without any religion whatever.[30] In cases of invalidity in which any of these exempt persons are concerned, they can convalidate their marriage by renewing consent privately. But they must have the knowledge that their marriage was invalid.[31] Parties may avail themselves of the concession of canon 1098. If they cannot have or approach the pastor or the Ordinary or a properly delegated priest to assist at the marriage, they may when danger of death threatens convalidate their marriage in the presence of the witnesses only; or even outside the danger of death if it is prudently foreseen that the Ordinary, the pastor or a delegate of either cannot be present to witness the marriage for a month.[32] Finally it may be noted in this connection that the form can be dispensed with when the convalidation takes place in danger of death.[33]

In all these cases both parties must renew their consent. If only one party gives the new consent the second union will be invalid from lack of proper consent. It is allowed, however, to substitute a proxy, who expresses the renewal of consent of the one whom he represents. In this case all the prescriptions regulating the use of a proxy must be observed.[34]

It may happen, in a rare case, that the impediment, though public, is not known to one or to both of the parties to the marriage. Must they in this case renew consent publicly? Unless a *sanatio in radice* is obtained both must renew their consent. The purpose

[29] Canon 1099, § 2.

[30] Canon 1099, § 2. Two replies of the Commission for the Interpretation of the Code declared that in this class are included the children of mixed marriages (July 20, 1929, II—*AAS*, XXI [1929], 573), and those born of apostate parents (Feb. 17, 1930—*AAS*, XXII (1930), 195).

[31] The law requiring the knowledge of the nullity of the marriage is binding upon baptized non-Catholics. Cf. Chapter III, Art. I.

[32] Payen, *De Matrimonio*, II, n. 2557, 3.

[33] Canon 1043; cf. Chapter VII, Art. I.

[34] Canon 1089.

of the law which imposes the public renewal is to make evident the fact that the marriage has been convalidated. Here then the marriage which was publicly invalid must be made publicly valid. It is the duty of the pastor if both parties are unaware of the impediment, or of the party who realizes the invalidity if only one is unaware, to inform the ignorant party of the invalidity and the necessity of renewing consent. With this knowledge both can give a new and effective consent.

In all cases of public convalidation the marriage must be recorded as soon as possible in the matrimonial register.[35] The obligation to make this record is incumbent upon the pastor of the parish in which the marriage is convalidated. He may do it either personally or through the priest who assisted at the convalidation.[36]

Together with the names of the parties to the marriage, of the witnesses, and of the assisting priest, there must be entered the notice of any dispensation granted for the convalidation.[37] It is important to remember this especially when the nullity of the marriage was due to an impediment. Usually a dispensation must be granted to make the convalidation possible. All this may be entered in the place of the former record of the invalid marriage, if it had been recorded. If that is not possible a new entry must be made together with a reference to the former record.[38]

Notice of the convalidation must also be inserted in the baptismal register if the parties were baptized in the parish in which the convalidation takes place; if the baptism was conferred in another parish (or parishes) notice of the convalidation must be sent to those parishes to be entered into the baptismal records there.[39]

But if the marriage is convalidated in a quasi-occult manner, that is, before the pastor and two witnesses only, and if the parties are generally thought to be validly married the record of the marriage is entered into the secret register of the diocesan curia.[40]

[35] Canons 470, 1; 1103; *Rituale Romanum*, Tit. VII, Cap. II, n. 6; Tit. XII, Cap. IV.

[36] Canon 1103, § 1; Cappello, *De Sacramentis*, III, n. 718, 3.

[37] Canon 1046.

[38] Vlaming, *Praelectiones Juris Matrimonii*, n. 771; Rossi, *De Matrimonii Celebratione*, p. 143.

[39] Canon 1103, § 2; Rossi, *De Matrimonii Celebratione*, p. 143, note 33.

[40] Cardinal Caprara, *Instructio . . . Circa Revalidationem Matrimoniorum*

Section 11

After an Occult Impediment

Canon 1135, § 2. Si sit occultum et utrique parti notum, satis est ut consensus ab utraque parte renovetur privatim et secreto.

§ 3. Si sit occultum et uni parti ignotum, satis est ut sola pars impedimenti conscia consensum privatim et secreto renovet, dummodo altera in consensu praestito perseveret.

In considering occult impediments, three hypotheses may arise: the occult impediment may be known to both parties, or only to one, or to neither. Each has its peculiar manner of convalidation. The Code mentions only the first two of these suppositions. It is presupposed by the Canon that the proper juridic form has been observed.

1. If both parties know their marriage is invalid because of an occult impediment it is sufficient if both parties renew their consent privately or secretly.[41]

An occult impediment is one that cannot be proved in the external forum.[42] Like public impediments, occult impediments may be divided into two classes, occult by nature and occult in fact. The former signifies an impediment which, considered in itself, cannot be proved in the external forum. Thus the impediment of crime resulting from adultery and promise of marriage is in itself an impediment occult by nature. It is occult in fact when the circumstances which are its source cannot be proved in the external forum; in this case the impediment is occult only by nature.[43] Only when the impediment which invalidated the marriage is occult both in nature and in fact can the prescriptions of the canon be applied.

After the impediment has been removed by a dispensation or

Nulliter Initorum—Zitelli, *De Dispensationibus Matrimonialibus*, p. 176, n. 6. Wernz-Vidal, *Jus Canonicum*, V, n. 413, 2; Payen, *De Matrimonio*, II, n. 2566, 1.

[41] Canon 1135, § 2.

[42] Canon 1037.

[43] Payen, *De Matrimonio*, I, n. 553, 4.

by a change of the circumstances from which it arose the parties must renew their consent. It is sufficient if they renew it secretly or privately. The reason for this is evident. The invalidity of the marriage is not publicly known and juridically, in the external forum, it is considered valid. Therefore no scandal has resulted from the invalid union or from the fact that the parties to this invalid union have lived together as husband and wife.[44] The knowledge of the nullity remains with the parties themselves. Hence they alone need to know of the convalidation. If they were compelled to convalidate their marriage publicly it is very probable that a new scandal would arise and they themselves would be embarrassed by the revelation that they had lived in an invalid union. Furthermore, the renewal of consent in the public form would not accomplish any good. The form was introduced by the Council of Trent to prevent abuses that came from clandestine marriages, when one person already secretly married might easily leave his lawful wife and marry another. In the case of the occult impediment there is no danger of this since the parties in the external forum are considered validly married. Any danger of a second marriage is removed by that fact.

This private and secret renewal is sufficient to convalidate the marriage. But it is not absolutely necessary that it be secret or private. If the parties therefore desire a public convalidation it may be granted to them. In this event it is necessary to prevent scandal that is possible from the renewal of consent in public.

The new consent is secret, that is, without witnesses; or private, without the prescribed form. But it must be made externally, that is, there must be a definite manifestation of it. Each must know that the other renews consent because each realizes that the first consent was not effective. Marital consent must be mutual, that is, each must give and accept the rights peculiar to marriage; and this giving and accepting must be known to both.[45] Since the consent given at the first ceremony did not produce this mutual exchange of marriage rights it must be done now by an external consent.

[44] Sanchez, *De Matrimonio*, II, Disp. XXXVII, n. 3; Benedict XIV, *Institutiones Ecclesiasticae*, Inst. LXXXVII, n. LX.

[45] Sanchez, *De Matrimonio*, II, Disp. XXV, n. 1.

The manifestation need not necessarily be in words.[46] Any external sign that signifies internal consent suffices. Words are the best means that can be used and it is the mind of the Church that they be employed when possible,[47] for she requires them for the lawfulness of the consent.[48] Ordinarily, then, they should be used in renewing consent but their use is not demanded under pain of invalidity.

Is the voluntary accepting and rendering of the marriage debt sufficient to express a renewal of consent? Can two persons who are aware of the invalidity of their union and of the necessity of renewing consent convalidate their marriage if they express the renewal of consent only by the free use of the marriage right? They can do so validly if they use the right *animo maritali.* The reason is that they both realize the invalidity and are convinced that they must renew consent before their marriage is convalidated. With this knowledge they can use the marriage right and consider it a sign, mutual and external, of internal consent.[49]

It is the duty of the pastor or the confessor to instruct the parties to an invalid marriage in the proper manner of renewing consent. He perhaps ought to ask them to exchange their consent in his presence or instruct them how to renew it in the presence of each other. An easy and effective way is to have the pastor ask each in the presence of the other if he and she accepts the other as wife or husband.[50] It might even be well if he were to use the words used ordinarily in the marriage ceremony for the exchange of consent. Thus he will make certain there is no misunderstanding and relieve himself and the parties of any scruples about the validity of the convalidation. As soon as the exchange has been made the marriage becomes valid; there is no need for anything more.

Must this mutual exchange of consent be made at the same time? Must both renew consent at the same moment? No, this is not

[46] Sanchez, *De Matrimonio,* II, Disp. XXXI, n. 5.

[47] Canon 1088, § 2.

[48] Cappello, *De Sacramentis,* III, n. 617.

[49] Payen, *De Matrimonio,* II, n. 2558.

[50] Cappello, *De Sacramentis,* III, n. 845; Gasparri, *De Matrimonio* (Ed. 1932), n. 1199.

required.[51] It is sufficient if there is a moral union between the time of the renewal of both parties. In practice this means that the consent of one must be joined to the perseverance of the consent of the other. Sanchez, without limiting the time,[52] insists that the period intervening between the two acts should not be very great. But since the actual perseverance of consent is all that is required and since consent will persevere until it is recalled, it may be stated that no length of time in itself revokes the consent. Hence regardless of the length of the interval, provided the consent endures, the other may renew consent and thus validate the marriage.[53] This is confirmed by the fact that the Church even after long years grants a *sanatio in radice*—which would be impossible if the consent did not persevere and remain effective for marriage.

However care must be taken that the consent does persevere and it is the duty of the party who has withheld consent to ascertain that fact. The longer the space of time intervening the more pressing is the duty of obtaining that knowledge. It might easily be presumed that the one who first consented has recalled consent if the other has neglected to renew his consent over a long period of time.[54] If one of the parties accepts the consent of the other but defers his own until some later time the convalidation of the marriage is suspended. During the interim the parties are forbidden the use of the marriage rights and must live as unmarried people.

2. In the second hypothesis the impediment is occult and known to only one of the parties. When this condition is verified, the convalidation is effected by the renewal of consent of the party who is aware of the impediment joined to the persevering consent of the other. The consent may be renewed privately and secretly.[55] Three things therefore are to be noticed in this convalidation, that consent be renewed by the party who is aware of the impediment, that it be a secret and private renewal, that the consent of the other persevere.

[51] Sanchez, *De Matrimonio*, II, Disp. XXXII, n. 3; Gasparri, *De Matrimonio* (Ed. 1932), n. 1199.

[52] *De Matrimonio*, II, Disp. XXXII, n. 7.

[53] Payen, *De Matrimonio*, II, n. 1602, 2.

[54] Sanchez, *De Matrimonio*, II, Disp. XXXII, n. 7.

[55] Canon 1135, § 3.

The one who realizes the presence of the occult impediment must renew his consent because he recognizes that the first consent was not effective and consequently that the marriage is invalid. Now that the impediment has been removed he is capable of giving a valid and effective consent and must do so. The necessity of renewing consent rests wholly with the law of the Church which has the power to regulate these matters for baptized persons even under the pain of invalidity.

The consent of the party who is ignorant of the impediment is not required to be renewed because there is no need for it. A consent which is a naturally valid act perseveres and will remain effective until it is recalled. Even though it was rendered juridically ineffective by the hidden impediment it nevertheless remains a valid act, psychologically and naturally. Since the Church does not require a renewal in this case it becomes also juridically valid when united to the renewed consent of the other party. This union effects convalidation. It cannot be objected that the consent is now directed towards a different object than formerly because the removal of the impediment changes it. Subjectively the consent has the very same object since in both cases the party ignorant of the impediment intended to contract a valid marriage—the effect now produced.

In this regulation there is a change from the law previous to the Code. It was formerly demanded that the party who knew of the invalidity of the marriage and who sought the dispensation must inform his partner that the marriage was invalid and both must renew their consent. "Dicta muliere de nullitate prioris matrimonii, et ita caute, ut latoris delictum nusquam detegatur," was the clause usually appended to the dispensations granted by the Sacred Penitentiary.[56] Authors argued whether this clause was imposed for the validity of the dispensation and consequently of the convalidation. Some asserted that it was merely an advice and not a true condition so that if it were not fulfilled because of a grave danger the dispensation would nevertheless be valid.[57] Others maintained that because the clause (*dicta muliere de nullitate prioris matrimonii*) was in the form of an ablative absolute

[56] Benedict XIV, *Institutiones Ecclesiasticae*, LXXXVII, n. LXXV.

[57] Sanchez, *De Matrimonio*, VII, Disp. LXXXII, n. 61; De Justis, I, Cap. VIII, n. 181.

it was a condition which had to be fulfilled for the validity of the dispensation.[58] All doubt was removed when, after the Council of the Vatican, the clause was mitigated by an addition which allowed the informing to be omitted in cases where grave danger might result from giving this information.[59] Under the present law there is no need to inform the other party of the impediment. The one thing necessary now is that the party who knows of the impediment and invalidity of the marriage, must renew his consent. He may do it privately and secretly without form and without any witnesses. The reason for this allowance is that the form has already been observed; the consent which was a naturally valid act was mutually exchanged and was thought to be valid in the external form. Therefore the marriage also was held as valid in the external form. Hence no public renewal of consent is necessary. Nor is there any necessity for renewing consent in the presence of the other party since the consent already given is considered valid by that party, and it cannot be proved to be invalid since the impediment is occult.

This consent may be manifested externally by word or sign or by the proper use of the marriage right, that is, with the intention of using it as husband and wife and not for the purpose of sinning. Even the continued cohabitation *animo maritali,* and fulfillment of marriage duties may be a sign of renewal of consent.[60] These signs are considered to express internal consent because the party who knew the first consent was ineffective could have departed from the other but of his own accord has remained.

But it is not absolutely necessary that the new consent must be manifested externally; an internal act suffices.[61] Externally the earlier formal consent is considered valid and by internal renewal it becomes objectively and effectively valid.[62] But here again it is

[58] Benedict XIV, *Institutiones Ecclesiasticae,* LXXXVII, n. LX; St. Alphonsus, *Theologia Moralis,* IV, n. 1115.

[59] Martin, *Collectio Documentorum Omnium Concilii Vaticani,* p. 176; Gasparri, *De Matrimonio* (Ed. 1904), 1406; cf. Chapter II, Art. 3.

[60] Sanchez, *De Matrimonio,* IV, Disp. 18, n. 2, 3, 5, 6, 7; Payen, *De Matrimonio,* II, 2564; Gasparri, *De Matrimonio* (Ed. 1932), 1200.

[61] Gasparri, *De Matrimonio* (Ed. 1932), n. 1200; Cappello, *De Sacramentis,* II, n. 3°, 6.

[62] Payen, *De Matrimonio,* II, n. 2559, note 1.

well for the confessor or priest whose attention is called to the situation, to have the party renew consent in words or at least by a very definite and explicit act of the will. It is the most effective means to avoid anxiety about the convalidation.

It is very important to note that this renewal of consent must be united to the still persevering consent of the other party. This is essentially necessary for the validity. The reason lies in the doctrine that only by consent can two persons effect a marriage. Therefore, if the consent of the party who is ignorant of the impediment has been recalled or for any reason does not exist at the time of the renewal of the other's consent there can be no convalidation. The very essence of marriage is absent. Once consent has been given however it is presumed to persevere until it has evidently been recalled.[63] This is a presumption of the law; it is not indestructible for any direct proof to the contrary destroys its value.[64] But until the contrary is conclusively proved the presumption that consent still exists stands. The reason is that both parties gave their consent at the time of the first celebration of marriage and particularly is this true of the party who did not know of the impediment to the marriage. This latter party unaware that the marriage was invalid probably did not recall his consent precisely because he was under the persuasion that his marriage was valid and therefore he could not recall the consent he had given. Under such circumstances it is only reasonable to conclude that he has not revoked consent. Perhaps he would have recalled his consent if he knew that his marriage was invalid. But this is only an interpretative intention and effects nothing, certainly not a revocation of his consent.[65] This presumption is not destroyed if the party has merely a desire, however strong, to be free of the marriage which he considers to be valid. A wish or a desire is certainly not the equivalent of a revocation of consent once positively given. The same must be said of dissensions and discords if they disrupt the married life; they do not in themselves constitute a recall of consent. Even if the party has secured a separation from the Church authorities and a purely civil divorce there is no

[63] Canon 1093; Sanchez, *De Matrimonio,* II, Disp. XXXII, n. 3.

[64] Canons 1825, 1826.

[65] *Circa Dispensationem in Radice Matrimonii*; *AAS,* I (1865), Append. VII, 191.

certain proof that the consent which was given has ceased to exist. For Catholics who are instructed in their religion they are at most indications that the parties desire no longer to continue their common life and wish to separate. But they are not certain indications of recalled consent. In the case of non-Catholics a civil divorce most often does point to a revocation of a previously given consent. Thus a Catholic woman unaware that her marriage is null because of an occult impediment of crime may desire to break the marriage. She may even declare that if she were free to leave her husband she would do so. Beyond that she may approach the civil courts and secure a civil separation and on that authority actually leave him. But in none of these cases can it be certain that she has recalled consent. Probably she has not because she is not aware that she can do so.

If the party whose consent must persevere attacks the marriage and asks for a declaration of nullity must he be considered as recalling his consent? During the course of the trial the consent is thought to persevere because there are no certain signs that it has been revoked and the party is still persuaded that he has not the right to revoke it.[66] Only when a declaration of nullity has been pronounced is the consent presumed to be recalled. Both parties are now convinced there is no marriage. The separation in the external forum is now complete and the parties are thought to conform to the sentence and recall their consent.[67]

Usually, therefore, the presumption that the consent endures is valid and will continue to be valid until the contrary is proved, for example, by the use of witnesses who can testify that the other at least externally did recall consent. It must be remembered, though, that this is merely a presumption and has nothing whatever to do with the objective truth of the perseverance of consent and consequently with the convalidation. That depends upon the actual existence of the consent at the time when the other party renews his consent. But because it is merely a presumption the party aware of the invalidity must not hesitate to renew consent. However, in a case in which there is grave doubt about the perseverance of consent it is not amiss to ask the other party questions which will lead

[66] Chelodi, *Jus Matrimoniale*, n. 168.

[67] Vermeersch-Creusen, *Epitome Juris Canonici*, II, n. 457.

to a certain knowledge of the existence or cessation of his or her consent.[68]

3. The third hypothesis supposes that the marriage is invalid because of an impediment that is known to neither party. This might happen if two persons marry without realizing they are disqualified by an occult impediment of crime. The confessor, should, if he judges it expedient, notify one of the parties of this nullity and direct him to renew his consent. If he does this, the case will fall into the class last treated—in which the nullity is known only to one party. If the impediment becomes known to both parties the convalidation falls into the previous class—in which the nullity is known to both. In revealing the impediment and in asking for a renewal of consent the confessor must be guided by the rules of prudence and in general consult the best interests of all concerned. If he foresees that the persons will not renew consent then a *sanatio in radice* must be obtained in order to convalidate the marriage.[69]

When the invalidity of the marriage has been occult and the dispensation has been granted and the renewal of the consent has been made in the internal sacramental forum, there must be no recording of that fact in the matrimonial register not even in the secret register of the curia. That entails violation of the sacramental seal of confession.[70] But if the dispensation was granted and the renewal made in the internal non-sacramental forum, the notation of the fact can be made in the secret register of the diocesan curia.[71]

Beyond these three suppositions, which are the usual cases, there are a few others that demand notice. The first concerns an impediment which in the beginning was occult, but in the course of time has become public. What is to be the procedure when this occurs? The impediment of crime, for example, which invalidated the marriage has become public because the parties themselves have divulged the knowledge of it. In this event the nullity of the marriage must be considered public and it must follow the rules regu-

[68] Payen, *De Matrimonio*, II, n. 2559.

[69] Payen, *De Matrimonio*, II, n. 2560.

[70] Canon 1047.

[71] Canon 1047; Payen, *De Matrimonio*, II, n. 1929.

lating renewal of consent after a public impediment. In the meantime before the impediment became public the consent may or may not have been renewed privately and secretly in the internal forum. If it has been renewed the marriage has of course been convalidated in the internal forum and remains valid. But very probably that convalidation has never been made public and in the external forum it must still be considered invalid. It is necessary to validate it publicly. Thus any scandal that may have arisen from its public invalidity is adequately repaired. Public convalidation is necessary also to avoid any conflict between the internal and the external forum.[72] The external forum in this case can be safeguarded by publishing the fact of the former private renewal of consent and thus make it public knowledge. If, on the other hand, the marriage has not been privately convalidated it must now be convalidated in the external forum according to the laws that govern public renewal of consent. The reason is that it is necessary to prevent scandal which arises from public invalidity.[73]

It happens, also, at times that an impediment which was public becomes occult. This is possible if the witnesses or the documents which might have proved the existence of the impediment disappear. The impediment of age, for example, which is usually public may become occult if the records of birth are destroyed and the persons who could have proved the age of the party have died or disappeared. It seems that in this case the impediment may be considered occult and the marriage which it rendered null may be convalidated as any other marriage whose nullity is due to an occult impediment. Since the nullity was public in the beginning, it may safely be presumed that both parties to the marriage are aware of the nullity and therefore both will have to renew their consent. But in this case it may be done privately and secretly. There is no scandal to be repaired since the impediment is now occult. Vermeersch [74] advises in this case the use of the form that is prescribed for "marriages of conscience." [75] His reason is that the canon requiring the public renewal for a public impediment suffers no exception. But it is difficult to see how even the form of

[72] Gasparri, *De Matrimonio* (3 ed.), n. 1407.
[73] Reiffenstuel, IV, Append. XIII, n. 610.
[74] *Theologia Moralis*, III, n. 829, 1.
[75] Canons 1104-1107.

"marriages of conscience" is necessary in this case. The impediment has become occult and it cannot be proved in any manner in the external forum. There does not seem to be any convincing reason for demanding the presence of a priest and two witnesses. It is sufficient if the parties renew consent privately.[76]

In case there is doubt about the publicity of the impediment it is more safe to renew the consent publicly. This accomplishes a two-fold purpose; if afterward the impediment should become public there will be no scandal and the proof of the marriage will be sufficiently established in the external as well as in the internal forum. However to save the parties embarrassment, because the impediment is at most only doubtfully public, the pastor may allow the parties to renew their consent in his presence and that of the witnesses only. In all cases of doubt the pastor should consult the Ordinary to insure the correct procedure.[77]

The following paragraphs contain the application of these rules under ordinary circumstances to the individual impediments.

A. Age. The impediment of age may be removed by dispensation because it is of ecclesiastical law,[78] or it will disappear with the passing of time.[79] In either case the consent must be renewed with the realization that the former union was invalid. Since the impediment is public consent must be renewed publicly. In an extraordinary case in which the witnesses and the records vanish the impediment may become occult and the consent could be renewed privately.

B. Impotency. Impotency which is antecedent and perpetual constitutes a diriment impediment to marriage. It may be absolutely perpetual so that it can not be cured in any way. In this instance a marriage which it nullifies can never be convalidated because impotency, being an impediment of natural law, can not be removed by dispensation. It is also considered perpetual (and therefore a diriment impediment) if it is of such a nature that it

[76] Wernz-Vidal, *Jus Canonicum,* V, n. 212; Payen, *De Matrimonio,* I, n. 965.

[77] Gasparri, *De Matrimonio* (3 ed.), n. 1407.

[78] Gasparri, *De Matrimonio* (Ed. 1932), n. 492.

[79] Dispensation from the impediment of age is conceded but rarely and then only for very grave reasons. Cappello, *De Sacramentis,* III, n. 338.

can be cured only by a surgical operation which seriously threatens life and health. In this instance the marriage it nullified can be convalidated if the person suffering from the impotency submits to the operation in spite of the danger, is cured of the impotency and renews consent. The other party will renew consent or not according as he is aware or not of the impediment.

C. *Ligamen.* The impediment of *ligamen* assumes an added significance due to the increase of divorce. Since the first marriage is usually presumed to be valid, it likewise may be presumed that a great number of marriages contracted after divorce are invalid. If the pastor after an investigation discovers that the first marriage was valid he knows that the second is invalid. Unless the bond of the first marriage has been broken in some legitimate manner, for example, by Pauline Privilege or by death, the second marriage can not be convalidated. If the bond of the first marriage has been solved legitimately the parties of the second may convalidate their union by renewing consent in the form prescribed by law. The public form is required because the impediment of *ligamen* is public by its nature.[80]

D. Disparity of Worship. The impediment of disparity of worship can be removed either by a dispensation or by baptism of the infidel party. After it has been removed both parties must renew their consent in the form prescribed by law because the impediment is of its nature public. If disparity is removed by baptism in a non-Catholic sect a dispensation from mixed religion is required. If the disparity is to be removed by a dispensation it is necessary that the non-Catholic party give the promise not to pervert the Catholic partner, and both must pledge themselves to have all the children baptized and educated in the Catholic religion only.[81] In convalidating such marriages there will often be question of the education, perhaps even of the baptism, of the children already born of the invalid marriage. Must they also be included in the

[80] In this connection the pastor must be wary of the impediment of crime which is contracted by those persons who commit adultery and attempt civil marriage. Not unfrequently the impediment of crime lurks in marriages which are attempted despite the impediment of *ligamen*. Cf. Canons 1075, § 1 and 1053.

[81] Canons 1071, 1061; Decree of the Holy Office, Jan. 14, 1932—*ASS*, XXIV (1932), 25.

promises? Authors generally are noncommittal on this subject. Some[82] require that the *cautiones* include those children that already have been born of the invalid union. But from the evidence that can be gathered there is no certain answer to the question, and therefore one cannot say with finality and certainty that the *cautiones* must include the children already born.[83] In any case, if the children have already been educated there is no necessity of demanding that the *cautiones* include them. If they have reached the use of reason no form of baptism can be forced upon them.[84] If they are not already educated or baptized it is safest in practice to include them because the dispensation will certainly be valid in this case. Moreover, it will insure the obtaining of the dispensation for despite the uncertainty of the law on this point some Ordinaries do not grant the dispensation unless the *cautiones* include the children already born. If the non-Catholic party refuses entirely to give the required *cautiones,* even though he is willing to renew his consent before a priest, there can be no simple convalidation. In this event the Catholic party must seek a *sanatio in radice.*[85] If this disparate marriage has been attempted before a civil officer or a non-Catholic minister, the Ordinaries of the United States have the faculty to grant this *sanatio,* provided the non-Catholic party is not *opposed* to the Catholic baptism and the Catholic education of the children, already born or to be born.[86]

E. Sacred Orders and Solemn Religious Profession. If the marriage is invalid because of the impediment of Holy Orders or of Solemn Religious Profession, the renewal of consent must take place publicly after a dispensation has been obtained from the Holy See. It is to be noted that only rarely are dispensations from

[82] Gasparri, *De Matrimonio* (Ed. 1932), n. 451; Prümmer, *Theologia Moralis,* III, n. 781; Payen, *De Matrimonio,* I, n. 1126, 3.

[83] For a discussion of this subject consult: O'Neil, "Extent of Guarantees in Mixed Marriages"; *IER.* XXII (1924), 417, 2. "The Promises in Mixed Marriages 'de Prole jam Nata,'" *AER.* LXXIV (1926), 630, 632. Schenck, *The Matrimonial Impediments of Mixed Religion and Disparity of Cult,* 238-245.

[84] Canon 752, § 1.

[85] S. C. S. Off., Decretum, Dec. 22, 1916—*AAS,* IX (1917), 13.

[86] Quinquennial Faculties of Ordinaries; Latest Formula for the United States—Bouscaren, *Canon Law Digest, Cumulative Supplement* 1935-36, Canon 66, pp. 5-6.

the priesthood granted; never, from the episcopacy. But after all such dispensations it is imperative to renew the consent in a quasi-secret manner, that is before the priest and the witnesses only.

F. Abduction. A dispensation from the impediment of abduction is very seldom granted by the Church.[87] The parties therefore will usually have to wait until the impediment has ceased according to the conditions of the Code, namely, that the woman abducted must be entirely separated from her abductor and that she dwells now in a place in which she is entirely free from the constraint formerly placed upon her.[88] This impediment is usually public and the consent therefore must be renewed publicly.[89] It may happen though that the impediment is occult and even may be so hidden that is known only to the abductor. For example, a man abducts a girl with the externally apparent intention of lust, but internally and unknown even to the girl he has the intention of forcing her to marry him. When this condition exists prior to the marriage it is sufficient for convalidation if the man renew his consent privately and secretly.[90]

It will be useful to ask here: can a man convalidate a marriage if he forcefully retains the woman to whom he is invalidly married for the purpose of having her renew her consent? Does the impediment of abduction arise in this case and thus prevent the convalidation of the marriage? An example will make the case more clear. A man and a woman have contracted an invalid marriage because of disparity of worship which disappears later by the baptism of the woman who had been the non-Catholic. But she now refuses to renew her consent, and the man forcefully detains her in his power for the purpose of making her renew it. In this case Payen [91] asserts that the impediment of abduction does not arise. Therefore the marriage can be convalidated. The reason advanced is that the situation here described does not fulfill the conditions required by the Code for the impediment of abduction.[92] The canon speaks of detention for the purpose of forcing

[87] Vermeersch-Creusen, *Epitome*, II, n. 350, 4; Payen, *De Matrimonio*, n. 1286, 2.

[88] Canon 1074, § 2.

[89] Gasparri, *De Matrimonio* (Ed. 1904), n. 1410.

[90] Payen, *De Matrimonio*, I, n. 1287, 1.

[91] *De Matrimonio*, II, n. 2573.

[92] Canon 1074.

the woman into a marriage that has not yet been contracted and not of a woman already united in an invalid union. In the example given the woman has freely entered into the invalid union and has freely cohabited with her supposed husband. Therefore the impediment of abduction does not arise. But if one considers the purpose of the law, which is to protect the freedom of consent, as well as to instill hatred for such a heinous crime,[93] one is inclined to conclude that the impediment is incurred in this instance. There is present here the very same reason for the violent detention as in the case of the canon, namely, to extort marital consent; and the result will be the same, the lack of liberty in consent. The same conclusion seems to follow from the words of the canon: "Quod ad matrimonii nullitatem attinet, raptui par habetur violenta retentio mulieris, cum nempe vir mulierem in loco ubi ea commoratur vel ad quem libere accessit, violenter intuitu matrimonii detinet."[94] Certainly according to this the impediment of abduction seems to be present. Even though the woman did freely consent to the union and freely lived with a man whom she thought to be her husband, she is unwilling to live with him now that they both realize there is no marriage and she is free to leave. She is being detained violently by him. This seems to fulfill the condition of the canon which states that the impediment is incurred if the woman is forcibly detained in a place to which she freely went. In another place, Payen [95] concludes that the impediment arises if a woman willingly accompanies a man for the purpose of marriage, but afterwards changes her intention and now is detained by him against her will; in other words there is violent detention. There is no essential difference between the two situations, both constitute forcible detention for the purpose of obtaining matrimonial consent. The impediment of abduction is present in both. The marriage, therefore, cannot be convalidated by a renewal of consent obtained under such conditions.

G. Crime. The impediment of crime of its nature is perpetual and can be removed only by dispensation. Such a dispensation is

[93] Wernz, *Jus Decretalium,* IV, n. 280, note 34; S. C. S. Off., Instructio ad Epp. Albaniae, Feb. 15, 1901—*Coll.*, n. 2101.

[94] Canon 1074, § 3.

[95] *De Matrimonio,* I, n. 1275, note 1.

not granted by the Church in cases which involve public homicide.[96] In other cases, the convalidating of a marriage is sufficient cause for granting dispensation from this impediment. The renewal of consent must be public if the impediment is public in fact. If it is occult (and this will usually be true) both parties must renew their consent secretly and privately unless the impediment is known to one party only. This would be verified if the impediment results from adultery and homicide but with the latter recognized as such only by the person who is guilty of it. He alone renews consent.[97] The pastor of souls must be on guard to detect this impediment in the cases in which persons have attempted marriage after a civil divorce and have consummated that marriage.[98]

H. Consanguinity, Affinity, Spiritual Relationship, Legal Adoption. If the marriage is null from the impediments of consanguinity, affinity, spiritual relationship or legal adoption, the renewal of consent regularly must take place in the public form, for these impediments are public by nature and usually in fact. Should they in an extraordinary case be occult the renewal may be made privately and secretly.

I. Public Propriety. The impediment of public propriety demands a public renewal of consent whenever it results from a public concubinage. But if it arises from an invalid marriage the renewal of consent will be secret and private if the knowledge of the invalidity is occult; but public and in the form prescribed by Church law if the impediment is public or if the knowledge of the invalid union is public.

[96] Benedict XIV, Ep. "Aestas," Oct. 28, 1757, ad XV—*Bullarium*, III, Pars II, p. 476; Gasparri, *De Matrimonio* (Ed. 1932), n. 683.

[97] Payen, *De Matrimonio*, I, n. 1372, 2.

[98] Canon 1075, § 1.

CHAPTER V

CONVALIDATION FOLLOWING DEFECTIVE CONSENT

Canon 1136. Matrimonium irritum ob defectum consensus convalidatur, si pars quae non consenserat, iam consentiat, dummodo consensus ab altera parte praestitus perseveret.

Si defectus consensus fuerit mere internus, satis est ut pars quae non consenserat interius consentiat.

Si fuerit etiam externus necesse est consensum etiam exterius manifestare, vel forma jure praescripta, si defectus fuerit publicus, vel alio modo privato et secreto, si fuerit occultus.

The convalidation of a marriage which has been null because of defective consent requires three things: the removal of the defect of consent, the knowledge of the nullity and the renewal of consent. The knowledge of the nullity, required by ecclesiastical law, has already been discussed. The present chapter is concerned with the removal of the defect of consent and the renewal of consent.

Article 1

Removal of the Defect

It is important to note immediately that defects of consent are not rectified by dispensations granted by Church authorities. Consent is the very essence of the marriage contract and therefore the Church is powerless to grant a dispensation which would exempt the parties to a marriage from furnishing this necessary element of consent. Without proper consent no matrimonial contract can exist. Nor can the Church grant a dispensation from this requirement of natural law in the event of a consent that is not entirely lacking but only defective, as she does in cases in which impediments of purely ecclesiastical law render the consent invalid and ineffective in producing a valid marriage. The reason is to be found in the fact that consent affects the very will of the contracting party, whereas impediments of ecclesiastical law are merely extraneous circumstances or external adjuncts which by the positive intervention of law disqualify the persons from obtaining the intended juridic effects of their consent. Such impediments exist apart from and are not essentially associated with the act of the will in itself. Therefore the Church can dispense from these disqualifying impediments unless they have been constituted by natural or divine positive law. But in the matter of defective consent the Church cannot dispense nor remove these defects. No human power can supply for them except those within whose will these defects have existed.[1]

Defects of consent are remedied in various ways in accordance with their nature. In many cases it is evident there can be no cure because the defect is permanent, e. g., permanent and incurable insanity. The subjects of these diseases, which undeniably impair the normal faculties of the will, can never make a valid human act and consequently are not capable of giving valid consent to marriage. Should persons afflicted with these or similar diseases exchange consent in a marriage ceremony it is without doubt invalid and can never be validated because the permanent nature of the malady imports the permanency of its nullifying effect.[2] If the defect is only temporary it may be cured sufficiently to allow the subject to make a valid act of consent. The source of those temporary defects may rest in the intellect or the will. On the part of the intellect the temporary loss of reason, ignorance and error may invalidate consent given under their influence. Although consent is properly an act of the will it depends upon the intellect for the material upon which or to which it is to make the act of consent, for nothing is willed unless it is foreknown. Anything therefore that affects the knowledge of the intellect interferes with the act

[1] Canon 1081., § 2. Because of the controversy relative to the divine or ecclesiastical origin of the law which constitutes fear as an invalidating agency in giving matrimonial consent, the conclusions here represented are in theory not absolutely final and definitive. But in view of the reasonable possibility and the acceptable probability that the law has divine origin, the Church in practice does not grant dispensations from defects of consent even in cases in which the marriages are to be convalidated. Cf. Wernz-Vidal, *Jus Canonicum*, V, n. 503.

[2] S. R. R., *Nullitatis Matrimonii*, Aug. 11, 1913, ad 2, 3—*S. R. R. Decisiones*, V (1913), Decis. XLVII; *Nullitatis Matrimonii*, Aug. 16, 1913, ad 2 —*S. R. R. Decisiones*, V (1913), Decis. XLVIII.

of the will. In the will itself force and fear, simulation and conditioned consent may render the act of consent ineffective.

If two persons attempt to contract marriage while one or both are suffering from a temporary loss of the use of reason the marriage is null because the consent is naturally invalid and insufficient to beget a contract. Thus a person who exchanges consent under the influence of perfect intoxication does not contract a valid marriage for he is not capable of making an effective act of consent.[3] Because these defects are only temporary they may be removed and indeed they must be removed before the convalidation of the marriage can be effective. It is very important in cases of this kind to make certain that the defect has been cured otherwise it will again invalidate the marriage.

Ignorance which vitiates matrimonial consent is the absence of knowledge that marriage is "a permanent society between man and woman for the procreation of children."[4] Since nothing can be consented to unless it is known, it follows that the object of the matrimonial contract must be known before valid consent can be given to it. The exact content of this ignorance is not definitely described by the canon. In general it is necessary that the parties know that they are contracting a marriage alike in its nature to that contracted by other people and as instituted by God. The realization that it is a permanent association of a man and a woman from which children are born seems to be sufficient for the validity of the marriage.[5] From this it can be seen that the existence of ignorance sufficient to invalidate marriage is difficult to prove.[6] After a person has reached the age of puberty this ignorance is not

[3] S. R. R., *Nullitatis Matrimonii*, Apr. 7, 1926, ad 5—*S. R. R. Decisiones*, XVIII (1926), Decis. XIV.

[4] Canon 1082, §1.

[5] S. R. R., *Nullitatis Matrimonii*, Mar. 17, 1910, ad 2—*S. R. R. Decisiones*, XVIII (1926), Decis. II, ad 6.

[6] S. R. R., *Nullitatis Matrimonii*, Mar. 17, 1910, ad 2—*S. R. R. Decisiones*, II (1910), Decis. XII. An example of the difficulty of proving that ignorance has invalidated marriage is a case tried three times before the Rota; cf. *Nullitatis Matrimonii*, Jan. 20, 1926, *S. R. R. Decisiones*, XVIII (1926), Decis. II in which the sentence was *non constare*. In appeal the sentence was reversed, *constare* (Aug. 2, 1929—*AAS*, XXII [1930], 185, 186, Decis. XLIII). Later (Nov. 10, 1930) it was again declared *non constare* (*AAS*, XXIII [1931], 102, Decis. LIV).

presumed to be present.[7] In any case it is necessary that the ignorance be dispelled before the marriage can be convalidated. It can easily be replaced by proper instruction on the nature of the sacrament of matrimony. After this has been given the marriage may be convalidated by renewal of consent.

Error nullifies consent but only under certain circumstances. It must concern the person of the other party or a quality so definitely associated with him that it is equivalent to an error of person.[8] Thus a man who intends to marry a definite woman is the subject of this invalidating error if unknown to him and without his consent any other woman be substituted for her; or again—if he has decided to marry one because of certain qualities which, to him, are essential to her and determine her in his mind and distinguish her from every other woman. If, for example, a man intends to marry the eldest daughter of a family whom he otherwise does not know he would contract an invalid marriage if another daughter presents herself and pretends to to be the eldest. The error in this case though it is only an error of quality is equivalent to an error of person.[9] The removal of the defect in these cases is accomplished by recognizing the error and correcting it, and renewing consent under the influence of this corrected knowledge.

On the part of the will consent may be vitiated by simulation, force and fear, and condition. Simulation is a pretense of giving matrimonial consent. Externally the party does give signs of consent but internally he withholds it either in part or entirely, by excluding some or all of the essentials necessary for marital consent. Thus he may exclude entirely the intention of entering a marriage, or he may curtail the rights which he is to give to the other party. If a man enters a marriage but excludes the essential quality of perpetuity by a positive act of his will he is giving only a simulated, and therefore an ineffective consent; or he may reserve to himself the right to limit the claim of the other party to the *jus in corpus* and thus exclude the *bonum prolis*. In these cases the marriages are invalid owing to the lack of proper internal

[7] Canon 1082, § 2; S. R. R., *Nullitatis Matrimonii*, Jan. 20, 1926—*S. R. R. Decisiones*, XVIII (1926), Decis. II, ad 7.

[8] Canon 1083.

[9] S. R. R., *Limburgen.*, Jan. 2, 1913, ad 2—*S. R. R. Decisiones*, V (1913), Decis. 1.

consent.[10] The cause may be removed by dropping all pretense and curtailments and by giving anew a consent that is sincere and entirely in accord with the intent of matrimony.

But in the majority of invalid marriages the defective consent is due to the influence of force and fear.[11] They may so disturb the will of the person that all deliberation and freedom are taken away, or they may merely lessen the freedom sufficiently to invalidate the consent. In the former instance the consent is invalid by natural law, in the latter by ecclesiastical law which requires that the consent be free from the influence of grave fear.[12] Before the marriage can be convalidated the fear must be dissipated. As long as the fear endures its nullifying effect follows. Even after long years of cohabitation and perhaps the birth of children the marriage remains invalid if the fear continues.[13] When the fear ceases to exert its influence upon the will the parties are capable of renewing consent.

In this connection a question arises: must the cause of the fear cease to exist or is it sufficient if the fear itself is removed? Sanchez says [14] that if the cause of the fear exists in its entirety the fear itself exists, despite the fact that the external act may appear to be free. Thus a person who has been forced by the threats of her parents into marriage cannot validate that marriage if the threats continue. But if they form only a partial cause of the invalidity of the consent and the other cause has ceased it seems the person can convalidate the marriage provided the fear

[10] Canon 1086; Gasparri, *De Matrimonio* (Ed. 1932), n. 814; S. R. R. *Nullitatis Matrimonii*, Mar. 8, 1913, ad 2—*S. R. R. Decisiones*, V (1913), Decis. XVIII; *Nullitatis Matrimonii et Dispensationis super Rato*, May 10, 1927, ad 4—*S. R. R. Decisiones*, XIX (1927), Decis. XXI.

[11] During 1935 the Rota passed definitive sentences upon eighty marriage cases. Of these forty were attacked as invalid on the ground of force and fear, and of these twenty-one were declared invalid. Cf. *Rotae Sententiae*—*AAS*, XXVIII (1936), 124-140.

[12] Canon 1087. The fear must be grave and unjustly caused by an external agent and the circumstances must be such that the party has no alternative but to choose marriage.

[13] For example, a marriage was declared null after seven years of cohabitation and the birth of nine children because fear was never absent even though the woman concerned had renewed consent. S. R. R., *Vicariatus Nyanzae Septentrionalis*, May 10, 1918—*AAS*, XI (1919), 89-93.

[14] *De Matrimonio*, IV, Disp. XVIII, n. 7.

itself has ceased and she is aware of the nullity of the former union. For example, if a woman is forced into a marriage with a man whom she detests it is evident that the detestation she bears him is at least a partial cause of the fear. If in the course of her invalid union with him that hatred is displaced by love the cause of the fear has ceased in part. It is not necessary that the threats of the parents cease (if the fear itself has disappeared) for they constituted only a partial cause.[15]

Certain types of conditions also nullify consent. Conditions may regard the past, present, or future. With the two former classes the marriage is or is not valid at the time of the ceremony according as the condition is or is not fulfilled.[16] If it is fulfilled the consent becomes valid immediately. If it is not fulfilled the consent itself is destroyed and the marriage does not exist. In this event the marriage cannot be said to be convalidated owing to the fact that there never was even an invalid marriage. Rather it is necessary of the parties wish to enter a valid marriage to contract an entirely new marriage. So also with the condition regarding the future if it is licit and not against the substance of marriage. The consent given is suspended until such time as the condition is or is not verified.[17] If it is fulfilled the consent becomes effective; if not, the consent is non-existant and no marriage results from it. Thus if a man enters marriage with the condition that he obtain a position in a few weeks no marriage is effected until that condition is fulfilled. If at the time specified the position is not obtained there is no marriage and the consent is recalled.

There are other conditions which not merely suspend the consent, but actually invalidate it at the moment it is given. Such are those conditions which, even though they look to the future, contain a stipulation contrary to the substance of the matrimonial contract or against one or the other of its essential qualities. Their invalidating effect results from this fact, that the consent to which they are added is not directed to the real nature of the marriage contract. It does not embrace all the essential qualities of its object as natural and ecclesiastical law define them.[18] It is of little

[15] Payen, *De Matrimonio,* II, n. 1695, 1°.

[16] Canon 1086, 4°.

[17] Canon 1093, 3°.

[18] Sanchez, *De Matrimonio,* V, Disp. IX, n. 3.

consequence therefore whether the condition be verified or not for the consent is null from the beginning and the mere verification of the illicit condition is not sufficient to render it valid. The marriage is null and can be convalidated only by withdrawing the condition and giving a new and valid consent.

Thus a man who contracts marriage with the condition that he will divorce his wife if the marriage is not agreeable to him does not give a valid consent and as a result the marriage is null. Whether or not he does divorce her later cannot change the nature of the marriage nor cause the consent to take effect. The consent was essentially vitiated from the beginning. The only resource the parties have if they wish to convalidate the marriage is to give a new and valid consent.

Suppose two parties between whom there is a diriment impediment of consanguinity enter marriage with this condition "if we can obtain a dispensation." Ordinarily a future condition merely suspends the consent which becomes effective as soon as the condition is verified. There is no need of renewing consent. But in the example cited the presence of an impediment casts some doubt upon the procedure to be followed after the dispensation has been granted. Must the two parties concerned renew consent? Vermeersch [19] maintains that consent must be renewed after the dispensation has been granted and the condition thus fulfilled. This, he says, is the common and the correct opinion and a requirement of ecclesiastical law. Wernz,[20] Gasparri,[21] Feije,[22] Chelodi,[23] Payen,[24] and Vlaming [25] agree with him in this contention. Sanchez,[26] Cappello,[27] and Vidal [28] assert, on the contrary, that the obligation to renew consent is at least doubtful. Perhaps a distinction is necessary. Natural law does not require this consent;

[19] *Epitome*, II, n. 381, 3.

[20] *Jus Decretalium*, IV, n. 297.

[21] *De Matrimonio* (Ed. 1932), n. 918.

[22] *De Impedimentis et Dispensationibus Matrimonialibus*, n. 647.

[23] *Jus Matrimoniale*, n. 126.

[24] *De Matrimonio*, II, n. 1738.

[25] *Praelectiones Juris Matrimonii*, n. 549.

[26] *De Matrimonio*, V, Disp. VIII, n. 10.

[27] *De Sacramentis*, III, n. 639.

[28] Wernz-Vidal, *Jus Canonicum*, V, n. 515, note 22.

almost all authors agree to that. The consent is naturally sufficient although it is suspended and ineffective. It is sufficient because even in the presence of the knowledge of an impediment a valid matrimonial consent can be given; [29] it is suspended because of the condition that has been added to it; and it is ineffective owing to the impediment which exists between the parties. But once the condition is fulfilled and the dispensation granted (both of which happen at the same moment), the naturally valid consent becomes effective and the marriage is convalidated in natural law. Is the effect the same in ecclesiastical law? Gasparri,[30] maintains that since the canon enjoins a renewal of consent to convalidate marriage which is null because of a diriment impediment the consent must be renewed. This, he says, applies to the case under consideration. But the argument is not wholly conclusive. First of all the canon refers to a marriage that has been contracted invalidly when the consent has been given absolutely but ineffectively, and not to a marriage that has been contracted only conditionally, when the effect of consent is suspended by a lawful condition. The correct solution of the question is that when the dispensation from the impediment is granted the consent becomes valid and effective for both obstacles to its effectiveness are removed at the same time. This seems to be a solidly probable opinion although neither side has definitely convincing arguments to offer. At best the case is doubtful. In practice there will be no difficulty for the rescript of dispensation contains the admonition that renewal of consent must be made. If however it be omitted in a particular case, the marriage will enjoy the protection of the law.

Article 2

Renewal of Consent

After the consent has been purged of all defects it must be renewed in order to convalidate the marriage. The definite question to be considered here is the manner of making this renewal. It varies according as the defect of consent existed in both parties or only in one of them, and whether it was public or occult, internal or external.

[29] Canon 1085.

[30] *De Matrimonio* (Ed. 1932), n. 918.

The lack of matrimonial consent may exist on the part of both persons or of only one. In the former case both must now give a new consent. There is no other means of validating the marriage because essentially marriage consists in the consent of two persons. If only one of them lacked consent he must now supply it. It is necessary in this latter event that the consent which is now given for the first time be united with the still persevering consent of the other party. Renewal is no longer required of the party who previously gave a valid consent which endures at the time of the convalidation, unless the defect of consent of the other party is public. Prior to the Code authors disputed whether or not this party also was bound by the law of renewal of consent. But the more common teaching was the same as that which is now in force.[31] The basis for the prescription of Canon 1136 is the principle that moral and not physical simultaneity in giving consent is necessary and sufficient to constitute marriage.[32] The only condition required is the perseverance of the consent of the first party at the time his partner renews consent. If that condition is satisfied the marriage becomes valid because the consent of both fulfills all the requirements for an effective matrimonial consent.

If the defect was merely internal the party or parties in whom it existed must correct it by an internal act.[33] The defect is internal when it remains entirely within the mind and will of the person who is affected by it, so that it is in no way manifested exteriorly. Such is the defect of consent given by a person who interiorly withholds consent while he exteriorly pretends to give it. The defect is known to himself alone. In this event the renewal of consent may also remain entirely occult. It may be entirely hidden, there is no need to manifest it to anybody not even to the other party of the marriage. Thus the person who has the duty to make the renewal may do so by an explicit act of his will, as "I take this person to be my wife." "I give now the consent that I withheld

[31] Sanchez, *De Matrimonio*, IV, Disp. XVIII, n. 2; Feije, *De Impedimentis et Dispensationibus Matrimonialibus*, n. 760; Benedict XIV, *Institutiones Ecclesiasticae*, LXXXVII, n. LXIX.

[32] Sanchez, *De Matrimonio*, II, Disp. 32, n. 3.

[33] Canon 1136, § 2; S. C. S. Off. *Instructio ad Vic. Apost. Oceaniae*, Apr. 6, 1843—*Collectanea*, n. 965; S. C. C. *Vigilien. Matrimonii*, July 13, 1725—Thesaurus, Vol. III.

before." Perhaps this is the safest way and the one best calculated to allay all scruples about the validation of the marriage. The confessor therefore to whose notice this case comes should instruct the penitent to act in this manner, not as a matter of necessity but rather of caution. It is not of necessity, because any valid internal act of consent suffices for convalidation.

Consent may be renewed also by properly fulfilling the duties of the married state, by the free and voluntary cohabitation, by the use of the marriage right, or, by any act that is usually considered an act peculiar to marital love and affection.[34] In so far as these acts are performed with the knowledge of the nullity of the union and with a will to consent to the marriage, they are effective for convalidation. But a person who performs these acts either without the knowledge that his marriage is null, or because he wishes either to sin or merely to preserve an external appearance of marriage, does not convalidate his union. His acts must be motivated and accompanied by marital intent (*maritalis affectio*), that is, the will of consenting to marriage.[35]

The Church does not demand an external act of consent in this case because it is not necessary. It was given in the first ceremony and therefore the purpose of the external consent has been entirely fulfilled already, that is, the establishing of proof in the external forum. For the rest the Church does not judge these merely internal acts.[36]

This rule of interiorly renewing consent applies to all cases of merely internal defect of consent whether it exists in one or in both persons.[37] Thus is settled a dispute which existed among authors before the Code. They argued whether in the event both parties have internal defects of consent both must renew their consent externally and mutually.[38] The present law requires only internal consent for both.

[34] S. C. C. *In Florentina Matrimonii*, July 29, 1854, § *quin-Thesaurus* CXIV (1854); S. C. S. Off. *Concinc. Occ.* June 12, 1850, ad 2—*Collectanea*, n. 1044.

[35] Payen, *De Matrimonio*, II, n. 2563, n. 2.

[36] S. C. C. *In Florentina Matrimonii*, July 29, 1854, § *quin—Thesaurus*, CXIV (1854).

[37] Wernz-Vidal, *Jus Canonicum*, V, n. 654.

[38] Cf. Sanchez, *De Matrimonio*, II, Disp. XXXII, n. 11; Feije, *De Impedi-*

But if the internal defect is so manifested that it becomes an external defect as well consent must be given externally in the convalidation. This is a logical consequence of the demand that the matrimonial consent must be legitimately manifested.[39] Since the defect of the first consent was external the required legitimacy of the manifestation was not obtained. Therefore its deficiencies must now be supplied. The manner of supplying them depends upon the character of the defect whether it was public or occult, and whether it affected the consent of one or of both parties.[40]

A public defect must be corrected by a public renewal. All marriages must be juridically valid in the external forum. But when there has been an external defect of consent the marriage is not juridically valid in the external forum, from the very fact that a public defect affords proof in the external forum that the marriage is invalid. In convalidation therefore it must be made evident that the marriage is valid in the external forum. Usually this publicity of renewal is obtained by the use of the form of marriage. Here it is prescribed by law under pain of invalidity.[41] The pastor therefore and two witnesses must be present at the convalidation.[42] It is to be noted in many decisions of the Sacred Roman Rota that marriages null because of public fear have not been convalidated, even after many years of cohabitation because there has been no renewal of consent in the proper form.[43]

mentis et Dispensationibus Matrimonialibus, n. 760; D'Annibale, *Summa Theologiae Moralis*, III, n. 484, note 23.

[39] Canon 1081, § 1.

[40] "Public" and "occult" have the same signification in this connection as they have when applied by Canon 1037 to impediments. Cf. Payen, *De Matrimonio*, II, n. 1564, n. 2; Cappello, *De Sacramentis*, III, n. 847; Wernz-Vidal, *Jus Canonicum*, V, n. 654.

[41] Canon 1136, § 3; Benedict XIV, *Institutiones Ecclesiasticae*, LXXXVII, nn. 62, 63; S. R. R. *In Causa Veszprimien.* June 2, 1911, ad 12—*S. R. R. Decisiones*, III (1911), Decis. XXI.

[42] This observance of the form is not obligatory upon those who are not obliged to the form of the Canon Law; nor upon those who in an extraordinary case are excused from it or dispensed from observing it. Cf. Canons 1099, § 2; 1043, 1044. Also Chapter VI, Art. I.

[43] S. R. R., *Parisien.*, Feb. 26, 1910—*S. R. R. Decisiones*, II (1910), Decis. VIII; *Tarvisina*, Mar. 11, 1912—IV (1912), Decis. XI; *Veszprimien.*, June 2, 1911—III (1911), Decis. XXI. These are but a few of many cases decided by this tribunal.

But it may happen that the defect of consent though external, is not public because it cannot be proved in the external forum. In this event the consent must be renewed externally but not necessarily publicly. Thus if two persons marry and they alone know that both acts of consent are defective, the defect is external but not public. They must make their renewal evident to each other by some external manifestation of it for each knows that the other's consent is defective. But there is no necessity for a renewal in the juridic form for in the external forum the marriage is regarded as valid. Consequently there is nothing to be gained by a public renewal. Indeed it might lead to scandal and to embarrassment for the parties if the form were to be used in the renewal.

Any word or sign that conveys to the other party the fact of a new act of consent suffices to fulfill the requirements of the law. Probably it is better to renew the consent in words to avoid any possible doubt about the convalidation.

How is a marriage to be convalidated if it is null from a defect of consent which formerly was public but now is occult? It has become occult, for example, because the only witnesses who could prove its existence have died. Since at the time of convalidation the defect is occult, this marriage is to be convalidated in the same manner as a marriage which is null from an external, though not public defect of consent. Therefore the renewal must be external but not necessarily public. Since proof of the invalidity of the marriage is lacking and impossible the marriage is valid in the external forum and there is no need to supply a public convalidation.[44]

A difficult problem in this regard concerns the convalidation of marriage by forced marital relations. The case is this: a woman has been forced into marriage against her will and now is forced also into *copula* with the man to whom she is thus invalidly united. Does such *copula* convalidate the marriage? Several hypotheses may be considered in this case. The fear which invalidated the marriage may or may not have been public and the woman may or may not have consented to the *copula*. If the fear has been public and as a result a public defect of consent has arisen the marriage cannot be convalided by mere *copula* even if the *copula* were freely

[44] Gasparri, *De Matrimonio* (Ed. 1932), n. 1203; Cappello, *De Sacramentis*, III, n. 848, II.

admitted by the woman. The renewal of consent requires the observance of the canonical form because the defect is public.[45] If the fear is occult the marriage ordinarily may be convalidated by *copula* which is freely admitted *animo maritali* by both parties. But if the *copula* is forced, and the woman consents to it as to an act of sinful intercourse, or if she remains passive and thus withholds all consent, the marriage is not convalidated. There is no matrimonial consent and there can be no marriage.

More perplexing is the case in which the woman who knows that her marriage is invalid and who, forced into *copula* by her partner, consents to it and to the marriage to avoid committing sin. A woman, for example, is threatened with serious dangers by the man who forced her into marriage unless she yields to his demands for the marriage debt. She consents to the act but fearing to commit an illicit act she consents to the marriage as well as to the act of intercourse in order that this latter act which otherwise would be sinful, may be legalized by the prior convalidation of the marriage. Is the marriage truly convalidated in this event? Chelodi, without making any distinctions, calls improbable the opinion which says that the fear ceases in such circumstances, and he maintains that this opinion has no value in the external forum.[46] This seems to be correct although it is not admitted by all canonists and theologians. If the fear has been public there must be a public convalidation in these circumstances just as in other cases of public invalidity. The law which nullifies consent extorted by fear is for the public good and not alone for the private good of the person forced into the marriage.[47] The object of the Church is her matrimonial legislation is to secure the most protection for marriage because it is a social and public institution. The private party entering into it, therefore, cannot renounce these laws even for his own advantage. In this event, then, the person forced must abide by the law which demands public renewal. Nor can it be objected that this is a case of grave necessity and therefore ecclesiastical law ceases. This does not excuse from the observance of the law here because the woman can, if forced to *copula,* remain passive

[45] Canon 1136, § 3.

[46] *Jus Matrimoniale,* p. 130, note 4.

[47] Wernz-Vidal, *Jus Canonicum,* V, n. 504.

and thus avoid the sin she fears.[48] Moreover, if the marriage could be convalidated by the consent given under the influence of the forced *copula* the result would be a marriage that is valid in the internal forum and invalid in the external forum. This is a contradiction that the Church in this case does not permit.

If the fear which nullified the marriage was occult under ordinary circumstances the consent could be renewed by the use of the marriage right. But if the marriage right were forced would the result be the same? It seems not. If marriage could be convalidated under these circumstances the nullifying effect of fear would itself be nullified by adding a second grievous wrong, the forced *copula,* to the first, the forced consent. This would soon render the law inefficacious for it would pave the way to all sorts of abuses in the matter of forcing the marriage debt to convalidate invalid marriages.

These arguments are not sufficiently decisive and definitive to settle the question but they do seem to establish the more solidly probable opinion.[50] However the opposing opinion must be considered probable because it is ably defended by eminent canonists.[51]

Would the addition of an oath to consent vitiated by fear validate the marriage? Under former law it seems that the marriage would remain invalid. Although this teaching was not unanimous, it was the more common opinion.[52] The Code does not definitely decide the question. For the following reasons it seems that the negative answer is more correct. The oath is concerned with a consent that is already essentially vitiated by fear. It cannot supply for these essential deficiencies nor does the addition of an oath in itself correct them. If it attests to a renewal of consent while the fear still exists and exerts its influence upon the will it certainly

[48] Chelodi, *Jus Matrimoniale,* p. 130, n. 4; Lehmkuhl, *Theologia Moralis,* II, n. 968.

[49] Cappello, *De Sacramentis,* III, n. 848, 1.

[50] Sanchez, *De Matrimonio,* IV, Disp. XVIII, n. 15; Schmalzgrueber, IV, Pars I, Tit. I, n. 416; Wernz, *Jus Decretalium,* IV, n. 268; Cappello, *De Sacramentis,* n. 848, 1; Chelodi, *Jus Matrimoniale,* p. 130, note 40.

[51] Payen, *De Matrimonio,* II, n. 1965; Gasparri, *De Matrimonio* (Ed. 1904), n. 929; Lehmkuhl, *Theologia Moralis,* II, n. 968.

[52] Sanchez, *De Matrimonio,* IV, Disp. XX, n. 12; Schmalzgrueber, IV, Tit. I, nn. 411, 412; C. 2, X, *de eo qui duxit in matrimonium,* IV, 7.

cannot validate it. That can be done only by purging the consent of the fear which invalidates it. Nor can the oath be considered a basis for believing that the consent was free because the oath itself is merely a accessory act and therefore follows the nature of the principal act.[53] In this case the principal act is the forced and therefore ineffective consent and the oath sharing in and taking its nature from this act consequently is also ineffective. One who can be forced into giving consent to a marriage is equally capable of being forced into swearing to a false oath. Hence it follows that the law invalidating consent extorted by fear would become ineffective and that force and fear would have no effective remedies in law.[54] In order to effect a valid marriage a man would be able, under the contemplated circumstances, to force a woman to consent to marriage and then, in order to validate the marriage, force her to take an oath attesting that the consent was freely given. Over and above this it must be remembered that the marriage laws of the Church are designed to safeguard the public as well as the private good,[55] and therefore the oath under consideration can have no effect because its private character cannot confirm an act whose consequences are detrimental to the public good.[56] Therefore it must be concluded that the oath added to a forced consent is not proof of the validation of the marriage.

[53] Accessorium naturam sequi congruit principalis. Reg. 42, R. J., in VI°. Cf. Canon 1318, § 1.

[54] Sanchez, *De Matrimonio,* IV, Disp. XX, n. 12.

[55] Wernz-Vidal, *Jus Canonicum,* V, n. 504.

[56] Canon 1318, § 2.

CHAPTER VI

CONVALIDATION FOLLOWING DEFECTIVE FORM

Article 1

Manner of Convalidation

Canon 1137. Matrimonium nullum ob defectum formae, ut validum fiat, contrahi denuo debet legitima forma.

The substantial form of marriage is prescribed by the Catholic Church under pain of invalidity. It requires that all marriages must be celebrated in the presence of the parish priest, the local Ordinary or a priest delegated by either of them, and of at least two witnesses.[1] Formerly a failure to observe the form of marriage prescribed by the Council of Trent in those places where the decree *Tametsi*[2] had been published was classified as the diriment impediment of clandestinity.[3] To day neglect of the form is not classified as an impediment but rather as lack of form. The source of the invalidity consequent upon it is the canon which imposes the form,[4] and not the law which governs impediments.[5] Any failure therefore to fulfill the requirements stated above results in an invalid marriage. There is no need for an impediment or a defect of consent. According to natural and Church law two persons may be capable to contract validly, they may have naturally valid consent, but if the form is not strictly observed the marriage is invalid from that source alone. If, for example, the priest who assists at a marriage is not competent because he is not duly delegated for this marriage, it is invalid, even though the parties themselves are entirely qualified to contract validly. Any essential defect of the form renders the union invalid whether the defect is noticed by the parties or the assisting priest or not. Thus if a

[1] Canon 1094.
[2] Council of Trent, Sess. XXIV, *de Reformatione Matrimonii*, c. 1.
[3] Gasparri, *De Matrimonio* (3 Ed.), n. 542.
[4] Canon 1094.
[5] Canons 1036, § 2; 1067-1080.

priest inadvertently assists at a marriage outside the limits of his parish it is invalid if he has not received the proper delegation.

Lack of form can render a marriage invalid only if the persons are bound to observe the form. All persons who have been baptized in the Catholic Church, those who are converted to it from heresy or schism even though they afterwards lapsed, and Catholics of the Greek Ruthinian rite,[6] are bound under pain of invalidity to contract marriage according to the form of the Code, whether they contract among themselves or with others.[7] Non-Catholics whether baptized or not, children of non-Catholic parents who have been baptized in the Catholic Church but educated from infancy in heresy, schism or without any religion whatever,[8] and Orientals except those mentioned above, are expressly exempted from the form of marriage by Code itself, when they contract among themselves.[9] But if they contract marriage with those who are subject to the form they are also bound to observe it.[10]

Those bound to observe the form may be excused from it either by dispensation or by concession granted by law in view of certain extraordinary circumstances which make the observance of the form morally or even physically impossible. Dispensation from the form may be granted in danger of death by any priest who assists at the marriage. Outside of danger of death dispensations from the form are not usually granted.[11] The law itself exempts from the form those who are so situated that they cannot observe it. Thus persons who cannot approach or secure the presence of the Ordinary or the pastor without grave inconvenience can in danger of death licitly and validly contract marriage in the presence of

[6] S. C. pro Eccl. Orient., *Decretum*, Mar. 1, 1929, ad 39—*AAS*, XXI (1929), 159.

[7] Canon 1099, § 1.

[8] The term "born of non-Catholic parents" includes also the children of parents of whom only one is a non-Catholic and those born of parents who have apostatized. Commission for the Authentic Interpretation of the Code, July 20, 1929, ad II—*AAS*, XXI (1929), 573; Feb. 17, 1930—*AAS*, XXII (1930), 195.

[9] Canon 1099, § 2.

[10] Canon 1099, § 1, 2°.

[11] S. C. S. Off. *Instructio ad Vic. Apost. Oceaniae*, Apr. 6, 1843—*Coll.*, n. 965; Ayrhinac-Lydon, *Marriage Legislation in the New Code of Canon Law*, n. 313.

witnesses only. Or even outside of danger of death when they forsee that the pastor or Ordinary cannot be present at the marriage and cannot be approached within a month, they may validly contract in the presence of the witnesses.[12] These marriages are valid, there is no need to convalidate them or even to supply the proper form later.

But if a marriage has been invalidated by lack of form it can be convalidated only by renewing consent according to that form. The parties to such an invalid marriage must exchange their consent in the presence of a competent priest and two witnesses, for the form prescribed for convalidation is always that promulgated by the Code.[13] It matters not when or where the previous marriage was contracted invalidly. Thus if two persons who were not bound by the law of the form contracted marriage invalidly in 1904 and only now realize that it is invalid, they must (if the form is required for convalidation) renew consent in the form prescribed by the Code. This is binding whenever invalid marriages must be convalidated with the observance of the proper form, regardless of the source of the invalidity.

The canon omits the distinction between occult and public invalidity and occult and public convalidation for the reason that lack of form is always by its nature a public defect and begets public nullity. Therefore the convalidation must always be public. But it may happen that the lack of form is occult in fact. For example, a priest, without obtaining the proper delegation from the local pastor assists at a marriage in a neighboring parish. If it is supposed that common error has not conferred the needed authorization the marriage is invalid. What is to be done? If the priest forsees that the parties will renew consent he should inform them of the invalidity and have them renew consent in the proper form but in a quasi-secret manner, that is, with only the witnesses and the assisting priest to witness it. The ceremony may take place, with the permission of the Ordinary, even in a private house because in this case there is present a reasonable and just cause.[14] This is done in order to prevent the scandal that might arise if the knowl-

[12] Canon 1098, 1°.

[13] Canon 1094; Vermeersch-Creusen, *Epitome*, II, n. 453.

[14] Canon 1109, § 2.

edge of the invalidity were made public. Sufficient publicity of law is obtained by the celebration of the marriage before the witnesses and the priest, and on the other hand publicity of fact has been secured by the previous observance of what seemed to be the proper form. But if the priest forsees that the parties will not renew their consent, or if he judges it is inadvisable to inform them of the invalidity he must ask for a *sanatio in radice* to convalidate the marriage.[15] If in this case the priest forsees that the nullity will become public in fact in the future it is his duty to inform the parties of the invalidity of their marriage and have them exchange a new consent according to the canonical form. This is demanded because the nullity which is public must be remedied by public renewal, and in the cases considered it is the only effective means of preventing future scandal.

It may be asked whether or not it is necessary to publish the banns of marriage before the convalidation is effected. Evidently not when the convalidation is private and secret; to publish them would defeat the purpose of the occult convalidation which is to avoid scandal to the public and embarrassment to the parties. If consent is renewed in the presence of the priest and the witnesses only the banns should be omitted for the same reason.[16] But if the nullity of the marriage and the renewal of consent are public the banns should be announced. However, in each case the pastor must decide whether the announcement is necessary and expedient. If he suspects any other impediments or obstacles to the valid or licit convalidation of the marriage he must announce the banns.[17] The expediency is usually judged by the possibilities of giving scandal to the public and embarrassment to the parties. If he is morally certain there is no impediment to convalidation and concludes it is not expedient to publish the banns he may petition the Ordinary for a dispensation. Convalidation of marriage, even of a civil attempt at marriage, is a sufficient reason for asking for this dispensation.[18]

[15] S. C. S. Off., Aug. 22, 1906—*Coll.*, n. 2239, ad 4; Gasparri, *De Matrimonio* (3 Ed.), n. 1449.

[16] Sanchez, *De Matrimonio*, III, Disp. IX, n. 9.

[17] Canons 1019, § 1; 1022.

[18] Farrugia, *De Matrimonio et Causis Matrimonialibus*, p. 134.

Article 2

Convalidation of Marriages Attempted before a Civil Officer or a non-Catholic Minister

Frequently pastors are asked to rectify attempts at marriage made by Catholics before a civil officer or a non-Catholic minister. These marriages are evidently invalid. They lack entirely the form prescribed by the law. It is only in an improper sense that these unions can be said to be convalidated for they have not even the appearance of a valid marriage. Yet it is imperative both for the good of the parties and the public good that they be rectified and the parties united in a valid marriage. Most often there are pressing reasons for asking for the necessary dispensations and even the necessity of rectifying a civil marriage is of itself sufficient.[19] Often the impediment of disparity of worship is present, frequently the impediment of crime resulting from adultery and attempt at marriage. It is incumbent upon the priest who assists at the convalidation to investigate the circumstances surrounding each marriage so that he may obtain whatever dispensations are necessary. Thus he will insure the convalidation against ineffectiveness. He must also ascertain if the party (or parties) has incurred the excommunication which is the penalty for attempting marriage before a non-Catholic minister.[20] If it has been incurred the pastor must make certain that it is absolved before the convalidation.

Is it necessary that these attempts at marriage be convalidated by the simple method? Can a *sanatio* be granted for that purpose? The reason for asking these questions is based upon the possibility that proper marital consent might have been lacking when the attempt was made. And since a *sanatio* requires that a naturally sufficient matrimonial consent must have been given it becomes doubtful if a *sanatio* can be granted.[21] Can a person (or persons if both are Catholics) give a true consent when when he is aware that the marriage will be invalid? The Catholic party usually considers the attempt at marriage as a mere ceremony, or as a means of ob-

[19] S. C. de Prop. Fide, *Instructio*, May 9, 1877—*Coll.*, n. 1470; Gasparri, *De Matrimonio* (Ed. 1932), n. 317.

[20] Canon 2319, § 1, 1°.

[21] Canon 1139, § 1.

taining more easily a dispensation, or of compelling his pastor to assist at a marriage at which perhaps he refused to assist in the beginning. If such is the state of the Catholic's mind he evidently does not intend to give a matrimonial consent at this first ceremony.

To solve the problem it is necessary to distinguish between theory and practice. Theoretically, true matrimonial consent is possible, This is true even though the party or parties realize that their act is forbidden and does not effect a valid marriage in the eyes of the Church. This is evident from the Code itself which states that a person's conviction of the subsequent invalidity of his marriage does not of necessity exclude his matrimonial consent.[22] Even in the face of the evident juridic nullity the parties may actually and truly intend by a naturally valid act to give and to accept the rights of marriage.[23] In this event the consent is truly matrimonial and the *sanatio* can be granted provided the consent still endures.[24] If one of the parties to the marriage is a non-Catholic it may safely be presumed that he has given a naturally valid consent. Usually non-Catholics are not concerned with the law of the form and they are convinced that the consent they give whether before the minister of their sect or a civil officer is sufficient to effect marriage. Consequently their consent enjoys the presumption of being valid.

But whatever may be the state of the question theoretically it is certain that there is no presumption in law to govern it.[25] Primarily and essentially it is a question of fact, and therefore must be treated practically in each case. The only presumption that exists is one of fact.[26] From these presumptions of fact the following conclusions may be deduced: (1) if the Catholic party (or parties) has been well instructed in his religion, if he has been taught the

[22] Canon 1085.

[23] S. C. Prop. Fide. *Respons. ad Vic. Apost. Constant.* Oct. 1, 1785—*Coll.*, n. 580; S. R. R., *Colonien.*, Aug. 27, 1910, ad 5, 7—*S. R. R. Decisiones*, II (1910), Decis. XXXI; *Argentinen.*, Feb. 23, 1912, ad v, xv—*Decisiones*, IV (1912), Decis. IX; *Argentinen.*, July 22, 1912, ad II, III—*Decisiones*, IV (1912), Decis. XXXII.

[24] Canon 1139.

[25] Chelodi, *Jus Matrimoniale*, n. 114.

[26] Payen, *De Matrimonio*, II, n. 1642; Wernz-Vidal, *Jus Canonicum*, n. 493; Vlaming, *Praelectiones Juris Matrimonii*, n. 530; cf. the Rota Decisions already cited.

sanctity of marriage and its sacramental nature and is acquainted with the Church laws on marriage and the prohibition against unlawful attempts at marriage, it is presumed that he does not give a valid matrimonial consent. He is fully aware of the futility of such a ceremony and recognizes that it does not beget a valid marriage.[27] (2) But if he was not well instructed, was remiss in fulfilling his religious duties and generally indifferent on matters of religion, it is presumed that he did give a naturally valid consent to contract marriage. He probably is convinced that this consent is sufficient to effect a valid marriage especially if it is a mixed marriage.[28] (3) If one of the parties is a non-Catholic, as usually happens, it is presumed that he did give a naturally valid consent. He is not aware that such a marriage is invalid, or if he has heard that the Church considers it so he is not convinced. He either disregards or disbelieves the teaching of the Church on this point.

These are merely presumptions and cede to the actual facts in each case. If both agree to renew consent there is no difficulty because the marriage can be convalidated by simple convalidation with the use of the public form. If one of the parties refuses to renew consent the pastor must ascertain whether or not both gave a truly marital consent at the first ceremony. If that consent was given and perseveres he may then apply for a *sanatio* to convalidate the attempt at marriage.[29] But if both parties refuse to renew their

[27] S. R. R., *Argentinen.*, Feb. 23, 1912—*S. R. R. Decisiones*, IV (1912), Decis. IX, ad 15.

[28] *Ibid.*, ad 16.

[29] He may apply to his own Ordinary for this *sanatio* "for marriages that have been attempted before a civil officer or a non-Catholic minister, . . . where there was the impediment of mixed religion or disparity of cult; provided that matrimonial consent continues to exist in both parties, and that the same cannot be legitimately renewed either because the non-Catholic party cannot be informed of the invalidity of the marriage without danger of grave damage or inconvenience to the Catholic party, or because the non-Catholic party can by no means be induced to renew consent before the Church or to give the promises as required by canon 1061, § 1, 2°; except in cases (1) where the non-Catholic party is opposed to the baptism or to the Catholic education of the children of both sexes already born or to be born; (2) where before the attempted marriage, whether that was private or public, the parties bound themselves to the non-Catholic education of the children as above stated: provided further

consent, the marriage is usually not convalidated; not by the simple convalidation because they refuse the renewal which it always demands, nor by *sanatio* for if both parties refuse to renew consent the Church usually does not grant a *sanatio*.[30] Such a marriage therefore will have to remain invalid and the parties, if they continue cohabitation, will be living in sin. In convalidating attempts at marriage, it is well to add that the pastor, in view of the leniency on the part of the law, should "strive with great charity and prudence to convalidate civil marriages that have been invalidly contracted." [31]

Article 3

The Liturgical Form in Convalidation

The liturgical form of marriage comprises the marriage celebration proper and the solemn blessing.[32] The rite of celebration of marriage as given in the Roman Ritual consists of the asking and receiving consent, the private blessing of the parties and the blessing of the ring. The solemn blessing which is given after the parties have already been married consists of the three orations which are pronounced over the bride and groom during the Nuptial Mass [33] or outside of Mass if the proper permission has been obtained. These are to be urged as the proper ceremonies to accompany marriages between Catholics. In convalidation, however, a number of distinctions are necessary to govern the use of the liturgical form.

It is evident that both rites are omitted when the convalidation is private or secret. These rites are of their nature public and are meant to be part of the public worship of the Church. Thus a man who renews his consent by a merely internal act or even by an external, though secret, act cannot make use of the rite of celebration

that there be no other diriment impediment for which the Ordinary has not the power to dispense or to grant a *sanatio*." *Quinquennial Faculties of Ordinaries: Latest Formula for the United States*—Private—Bouscaren, *Canon Law Digest, Cumulative Supplement*, 1935-36, pp. 5, 6.

[30] Farrugia, *De Matrimonio et Causis Matrimonialibus*, p. 493.

[31] Wernz-Vidal, *Jus Canonicum*, n. 595.

[32] Vlaming, *Praelectiones Juris Matrimonii*, n. 610.

[33] Canon 1101, § 1; Missale Romanum, *Missa pro Sponso et Sponsa*.

nor of the blessing. The same is to apply when both parties renew consent privately and secretly. There is nothing, however, to prevent their receiving the blessing later in their married life if they care to do so.[34]

But if the renewal of consent is made in the proper juridical form it should be accompanied by the marriage ceremony as it is found in the Ritual, with this exception [35] that if the ring had been blessed at a former ceremony it is not blessed again. A new ring, or one that is not already blessed does receive a blessing at the convalidation ceremony.[36]

If the consent is renewed in a quasi-private manner, i. e., in the presence of the pastor and the witnesses only, the ceremonies of the Ritual may or may not be used. Noldin seems [37] to imply that they should be omitted and that the pastor should be content to ask and receive the consent of the parties. But with Payen [38] it should be noted that there is no evident reason for the necessary omission of the ceremonies. Therefore their use or omission depends upon the parties and the pastor since they are not prescribed even for the liceity of the convalidation.[39]

A more difficult question concerns the giving of the solemn blessing in convalidation. It is certain that if it had not been given to the woman before in any ceremony of marriage it may be given now during the Nuptial Mass at the convalidation, or outside the Mass with special permission.[40] It is certain, too, that if the marriage is a mixed marriage whether by disparity of worship or mixed religion the blessing cannot be given.[41] But if the convalidation concerns a marriage between two Catholics who have already received the blessing in a former Nuptial Mass can the blessing be repeated in the convalidation? Some authors,[42] whose opinion has

[34] Canon 1101.

[35] Vlaming, *Praelectiones Juris Matrimonii*, n. 771; Gasparri, *De Matrimonio* (3 Ed.), n. 1402; Payen, *De Matrimonio*, II, n. 2566, 2.

[36] Gasparri, *De Matrimonio* (3 Ed.), n. 1231.

[37] *Summa Theologiae Moralis*, n. 664.

[38] *De Matrimonio*, II, 2566, 1.

[39] Cerato, *Matrimonium*, n. 139, b.

[40] S. C. Inq., Feb. 1, 1871—*Coll.*, n. 1557.

[41] Canon 1102, § 2.

[42] Sanchez, *De Matrimonio*, VII, Disp. LXXXII, n. 26; Wernz-Vidal, *Jus Canonicum*, V, 680, n. 25; Payen, *De Matrimonio*, II, 2641.

been termed more probable[43] maintain that the solemn blessing cannot be repeated whether the convalidation be effected during or outside of Mass. The blessing, they say, has been given once and it is given directly to the persons, not to the marriage. Therefore it remains with these persons despite the fact that it was bestowed during an invalid marriage. The proof that it is given directly to the person is that the law allows it to be given only once to a woman. Thus a woman who contracts two successive valid marriages is not allowed to receive the blessing twice.[44] In the case under consideration the blessing, even though it was given at an invalid marriage, is in itself valid and therefore still remains with those whose marriage is being convalidated. It cannot therefore be repeated.[45]

Other canonists more correctly assert that the solemn blessing can be bestowed at the convalidation.[46] The blessing, they admit, is directed to the persons, especially to the woman, rather than to the marriage itself and once she has validly received it the blessing cannot be repeated. But the marriage is a condition for its reception. It can be given only after the marriage has been actually and validly contracted for it is directed both by its terms and its meaning to married women. When it is pronounced during Mass the marriage has already been contracted either validly or invalidly; if validly, the blessing is received by the couple; if invalidly, the blessing is not received because they are actually not married and therefore not properly qualified to receive it. In the light of these considerations it would seem certain that the solemn nuptial blessing can be given at the convalidation of marriage. Since it may be given the delicate sense of pastoral duty will recommend its bestowal.

[43] Gasparri, *De Matrimonio* (3 Ed.), n. 1402. In a previous edition he asserts the affirmative opinion is more probable. *De Matrimonio* (Ed. 1892), n. 1130.

[44] C. 3, X, *de secundis nuptiis,* IV, 21; Canon 1143.

[45] Wernz-Vidal, *Jus Canonicum,* V, 680.

[46] Schmalzgrüber, IV, Pars IV, Tit. XXI, n. 43; Vlaming, *Praelectiones Juris Matrimonii,* n. 771.

CHAPTER VII

CONVALIDATION IN EXTRAORDINARY CIRCUMSTANCES

ARTICLE 1

In Danger of Death

Canon 1043. Urgente mortis periculo, locorum Ordinarii, ad consulendum conscientiae, et, si casus ferat, legitimationi prolis, possunt tum super forma in matrimonii celebratione servanda, tum super omnibus et singulis impedimentis iuris ecclesiastici, sive publicis sive occultis, etiam multiplicibus, exceptis impedimentis provenientibus ex sacro presbyteratus ordine et ex affinitate in linea recta, consummato matrimonio, dispensare proprios subitos ubique commorantes et omnes in proprio territorio actu degentes, remoto scandalo, et si dispensatio concedatur super cultus disparitate aut mixta religione, praestitis consuetis cautionibus.

Canon 1044. In eisdem rerum adjunctis de quibus in can. 1043 et solum pro casibus in quibus ne loci quidem Ordinarius adiri possit, eadem dispensandi facultate pollet tum parochus, tum sacerdos qui matrimonio, ad normam can. 1098, n. 2, assistit, tum confessarius, sed hic pro foro interno in actu sacramentalis confessionis tantum.

These canons restate more clearly and more definitely powers that were granted for the first time by Pope Leo XIII.[1] Before that time no such generous faculties had been granted by the general law,[2] though it was the common teaching among canonists that Bishops could dispense (to convalidate marriage) under certain conditions in extraordinary circumstances.[3] Summarized, these

[1] S. C. S. Off., *Encyc. Litt.*, Feb. 20, 1888—*Coll.*, n. 1685; *Fontes*, n. 1109.

[2] Cf. S. C. S. Off., *Instructio*, June 8, 1756—*Coll.*, n. 399.

[3] Reiffenstuel, IV, Append. *De Dispensatione*, n. 15; Gasparri, *De Matrimonio* (Ed. 1904), n. 440; Sanchez, II, Disp. XL, n. 3; Wernz, *Jus Canonicum*, IV, n. 618; Benedict XIV, *De Synodo Dioecesano*, IX, Cap. II, n. 1.

conditions were: that the marriage must have been contracted and solemnized *in facie ecclesiae,* and in good faith; it must have been consummated; there must be no time for recourse to the Holy See, and there must be the impossibility of separation without scandal.[4] But it was not until 1888 that these extensive powers became part of the law of the Church by a grant of the Holy Office.[5] At that time Ordinaries were granted the power to dispense in danger of death from practically all impediments except the sacred priesthood and affinity in direct line resulting from a consummated marriage. This grant of power forms the basis of the present faculties given by the Code of Canon Law. It has been amended, explained and amplified by official declarations of the Holy See between the time it was first granted and of its embodiment in the Code.[6]

The first comment to be made on the canon is that it is to be broadly interpreted. The Ordinary or priest who assists at such a death bed convalidation[7] must interpret the powers and the conditions in that manner and must not be scrupulous in the exercise of these faculties. They have been granted for the purpose of making secure in the last few moments of life, the eternal salvation of souls that perhaps are in sin. This must be seriously taken into account by the priest who assists and his judgments must be guided by that consideration.

The canon places several conditions that must be verified before the powers can be exercised. Danger of death must be present; scandal must be removed; peace of conscience or if there is occasion

[4] Benedict XIV, *loc. cit.*

[5] "Locorum Ordinarii dispensare valeant per se sive per ecclesiasticam personam sibi benevisam aegrotos in gravissimo mortis periculo constitutos, quando non suppetit tempus recurrendi ad Sanctam Sedem, super impedimentis quantumvis publicis matrimonium jure ecclesiastico dirimentibus, excepto sacro Presbyteratus Ordine, et affinitate lineae rectae ex copula licita proveniente." *Encyc. Litt.*, Feb. 20, 1888—*Coll.*, n. 1685; *Fontes*, n. 1109.

[6] For example: S. C. S. Off., Apr 23, 1890—*Coll.*, n. 1828; *Colocen.* May 25, 1898—*Coll.*, n. 2001; Apr. 12, 1899—*Coll.*, n. 2042; Dec. 13, 1899—*Coll.*, n. 2072.

[7] Though there is no direct and express statement in the canon that these powers may be applied to convalidation in danger of death it is evident that they do extend to that situation. Gasparri, *De Matrimonio* (Ed. 1932), n. 396.

for it the legitimation of children, must furnish the motive; and whenever necessary, the *cautiones* must be obtained. In the event of convalidation it is of course presupposed that a previous invalid marriage should have been attempted.[8]

The first condition stipulated by the canon is likelihood of death. It demands a condition of affairs in which it is probable that the person will die. It does not demand that there be certainty of death, nor yet that the person be "on the point of death." What is required is a prudent judgment on the part of the assisting priest that death probably will follow.[9] It is not necessary that the party who is directly affected by the impediment should be threatened by the danger of death. For example, the impediment of age may exist only on the part of the girl, while the danger of death may threaten the man to whom she is invalidly married. In this instance the power to dispense may be validly exercised.[10]

Besides danger of death the canon demands that there be a cause for the use of the faculty. Two causes are mentioned, either of which is sufficient and one of which is necessary for the validity of the dispensation. The causes are, the securing of peace of conscience for the parties and (if the situation so requires) the legitimation of children who may have been born or conceived during the invalid marriage.[11] Usually both of these causes are present in the death-bed convalidation of marriage although either one in itself is sufficient to warrant the valid use of these extraordinary faculties.

It is necessary for the lawfulness, but not for the validity, of the dispensation to insist upon the necessary precautions to guard against scandal which may easily arise from the circumstances which surround these convalidations. The means to be employed must be accommodated to the peculiar circumstances in each case.

[8] The commentary of this canon will be limited to the essentials and in so far as it applies to convalidation. For a detailed and expert explanation consult O'Keefe, *Matrimonial Dispensations, Powers of Bishops, Priests and Confessors*, pp. 55-124; Catholic University of America Canon Law Studies, no. 45; Washington, 1927.

[9] S. C. de Sacr., *Parmen. et aliarum*, May 15, 1909—*AAS*, I (1909), 468; Gasparri, *De Matrimonio* (Ed. 1932), n. 393.

[10] S. C. S. Off., July 1, 1891—*Coll.*, n. 1758.

[11] Gasparri, *De Matrimonio* (Ed. 1932), n. 394; Capello, *De Sacramentis*, III, n. 231, 2, d; Payen, *De Matrimonio*, II, n. 646, 2.

A very important prescription of the canon concerns the necessity of demanding the *cautiones* in all cases which involve the impediments of mixed religion or disparity of worship. Even in this extreme case the giving of the *cautiones* is essential to the validity of the dispensation. The Holy Office has insisted upon this in a decree of January 14, 1932.[12]

When the conditions described are verified the power to dispense is given to local Ordinaries (*Ordinarii locorum*), to pastors, to priests who otherwise might not be competent to assist validly at the marriage but are called to assist in danger of death when the pastor or other duly authorized priest cannot be present,[13] and to confessors, but only for the confessional forum.[14] Priests and confessors receive these faculties only when it is impossible to reach the local Ordinary without a delay that might prove dangerous.[15]

A question presents itself in the matter of the dispensations granted by the confessor. Since his power is valid only for the internal sacramental forum it seems that he may dispense only from impediments which are occult. Can he also dispense from public impediments in this extreme case of danger of death? Chelodi,[16] Veermersch,[17] and Augustine [18] maintain that the confessor can dispense from a public impediment even though his power is limited to the act of confession. Gasparri,[19] Wernz-Vidal,[20] Cappello,[21] and Vlaming,[22] restrict the confessor's powers to impediments that are occult by nature and in fact. In view of this disputed interpretation and also because the first opinion is termed probable [23] the confessor can, in virtue of the principle of canon 15 governing all doubtful canonical laws, validly dispense from all impediments except those expressly excluded by the canon.[24] But

[12] *AAS*, XXIX (1932), 25; Gasparri, *De Matrimonio* (Ed. 1932), n. 395.

[13] Canon 1098, 1, 2.

[14] In danger of death every priest may be a valid confessor to the sick person. Canon 882.

[15] Cf. Art. II, of this chapter.

[16] *Jus Matrimoniale*, n. 44.

[17] *Epitome*, II, n. 312.

[18] *A Commentary on Canon Law*, V, 103, 104.

[19] *De Matrimonio* (Ed. 1932), n. 398.

[20] *Jus Canonicum*, V, n. 428.

[21] *De Sacramentis*, III, n. 238.

[22] *Praelectiones Juris Matrimonii*, 414.

[23] Payen, *De Matrimonio*, I, n. 673.

[24] Augustine, *A Commentary on Canon Law*, V, 103, 104; Ayrhinac-

if he does dispense he must remember that his dispensation and the subsequent convalidation are valid only in the internal sacramental forum and therefore he must advise the parties (if he has dispensed from a public impediment, e. g., consanguinity) to make public the fact of the dispensation to the Pastor or the Ordinary so that both the dispensation and the convalidation may be made valid in the external forum. This obligation is grave because of the danger there is that later on the parties if they do not validate their marriage publicly may attack its nullity in the external forum, in which forum it must still be regarded as invalid. Therefore there is the possibility of nullifying juridically a marriage which is objectively and in the internal forum valid.[25] In danger of death these difficulties will be obviated if the confessor advises the penitent to manifest the impediment to the pastor or some other competent priest or to the confessor himself outside the act of confession, if no competent priest can be had, in order thus to secure a dispensation that will be valid both in the internal and the external forum.[26]

Most pertinent it is to remark that these powers, ample as they are, do not grant priests the faculty of conceding a *sanatio in radice*.[27] This was the accepted interpretation before the New Code was promulgated,[28] nothing in the canon warrants a change of interpretation. Nowhere does it grant that power either explicitly or implicitly. Nor does it empower the priest to dispense from the renewal of consent. Therefore, even in these extreme cases the convalidation must always be simple, and consequently the consent always must be renewed. The manner of renewing consent is to be guided by the rules given above and depends upon the nature of the impediment. There may be one exception. If it is a public impediment or a public defect that nullifies the mar-

Lydon, *Marriage Legislation in the New Code of Canon Law*, p. 73; O'Keefe, *Matrimonial Dispensations, Powers of Bishops, Priests and Confessors*, pp. 118-124.

[25] Ayrhinac-Lydon, *Marriage Legislation in the New Code of Canon Law*, p. 73.

[26] Wernz-Vidal, *Jus Canonicum*, V, n. 428, note 93.

[27] Gasparri, *De Matrimonio* (Ed. 1932), n. 396; Wernz-Vidal, *Jus Canonicum*, V, 413; Cappello, *De Sacramentis*, III, n. 231, 2, 1.

[28] Wernz, *Jus Decretalium*, IV, n. 617, note 67; S. C. S. Off., July 6, 1898—*Coll.*, n. 2007.

riage, convalidation may be effected without the observance of the canonical form. Ordinarily the form is required. But the priest who assists at death-bed convalidations receives the power to dispense from the form and thus may allow the marriage to be contracted or convalidated privately and secretly. In order to grant this dispensation it is necessary to have a reasonable, though not necessarily a very grave cause.[29]

Article 2

Outside Danger of Death

Canon 1045. § 1. Possunt Ordinarii locorum, sub clausulis in fine can. 1043 statutis, dispensationem concedere super omnibus impedimentis de quibus in cit. can. 1043, quoties impedimentum detegatur, cum omnia iam parata sunt ad nuptias, nec matrimonium sine probabili gravis periculo differri possit usque dum a Sancta Sede dispensatio obtineatur.

§ 2. Haec facultas valeat quoque pro convalidatione matrimonii iam contracti, si periculum sit in mora nec tempus suppetat recurrendi ad Sanctam Sedem.

§ 3. In iisdem rerum adjunctis, eadem facultate gaudeant omnes de quibus in can. 1044, sed solum pro casibus occultis in quibus ne loci quidem Ordinarius adiri possit, vel nonnisi cum periculo violationis secreti.[30]

The conditions of this canon are verified as often as the marriage which has been invalidly contracted must be convalidated immediately, that is, whenever it cannot be postponed without probable danger of serious evil to the parties until a dispensation has been received from the proper superior.

The first condition required is a state of affairs which makes the

[29] Ayrinhac-Lydon, *Marriage Legislation in the New Code of Canon Law* (Ed. 1934), n. 72.

[30] The commentary of this canon will be confined to those remarks pertinent to convalidation, though the canon is not meant merely nor even primarily for that purpose. For a detailed commentary reference is again made to O'Keefe, *Matrimonial Dispensations, Powers of Bishops, Priests, and Confessors*, pp. 129-186.

convalidation an urgent necessity. This is verified, for example, in the case in which two people are living together in an invalid union; they cannot be separated without danger to their reputation in the estimation of those who consider them validly married, nor can they continue to live together without danger of sin. This evidently is an urgent reason for convalidating marriage. Or again, if the parties in an invalid union desire to contract marriage so that the child about to be born will be legitimate, and a dispensation cannot be obtained from the local Ordinary before the birth of the child.[31] Or the urgency may press only on the one party. If, for example, the wife alone is aware of the invalidity of the union and cannot on the one hand refuse the marriage debt without revealing the invalidity to her husband, and on the other cannot allow the use of the marriage right without sin, there is an urgent reason for the dispensation. The pastor or the confessor can in this case dispense validly so that she may renew her consent effectively.

The probability of the danger is to be judged prudently by him who grants the dispensation. The circumstances of each case must be reckoned with, there can be no set rule. The danger itself may be either physical or spiritual, such as corporal punishment, scandal or sin.[32]

So also, the difficulty and the impossibility of the recourse must be judged by the one who grants the dispensation. The judgment is based upon the ordinary circumstances of such recourse and the means usually employed and considered by all as ordinary, v. g., by means of letter or personal approach.[33] The Holy See has continually considered the use of the telephone and telegraph as extraordinary means and therefore these need not, and in most cases, should not be used, because they are unsafe.[34] If therefore the

[31] Ayrhinac-Lydon, *Marriage Legislation in the New Code of Canon Law*, n. 77.

[32] Reiffenstuel, IV, Append. nn. 47, 49.

[33] The time usually allowed for transmitting a petition to the Holy See from the United States and receiving the rescript in return is forty or fifty days. Cappello, *De Sacramentis*, III, n. 234, 6.

[34] Cf. Letter of Card. Sec'y of State Rampolla to the Bishops of France, Dec. 10, 1891—*N. R. T.*, XXIV (1892), 32, 33; Litt. Sec. Stat. Episcopo Argentinensi, Jan. 5, 1892—*AAS*, XXIV (1892), 447; S. C. S. Off., *Dubium*, Aug. 14, 1892—*ASS*, XXIX (1901), 642; Reply of the Pontifical Com-

priest who assists at the marriage or its convalidation prudently judges that under the circumstances ordinary recourse is not possible without a danger to the parties concerned he may validly dispense from all impediments except those excluded by the canon itself, that is, all impediments of ecclesiastical law except those arising from the priesthood or from affinity in the direct line when the marriage from which it arises has been consummated.

It is important to notice that the form of marriage is not included in these extensive powers. If therefore the convalidation calls for the renewal of consent in the canonical form, the form must be used. If the nullity of the marriage has been occult the renewal takes place in a secret and private manner, not in virtue of a dispensation, which cannot be granted under this canon, but in accord with the laws of convalidation which do not require the form in these circumstances. Thus if a pastor discovers that two persons are living in a marriage invalid because of the impediment of crime but which was contracted in the canonical form, he may if the conditions of the canon are verified dispense from the impediment and have the persons renew their consent privately.

The power of dispensing given to priests in such extraordinary circumstances is limited to occult cases, that is, those in which the impediment and the nullity have been hidden. It had been disputed whether "occult" here referred only to those cases that are occult both in fact and by nature, or if it included also those that are occult in fact, though public by nature. The dispute was settled by a decision of the Commission for the Interpretation of the Code, December 28, 1927.[35] It decided that the phrase *pro casibus occultis* in the canon refers also to those cases in which the impediment is public by nature and occult in fact.

The important observation to be made in this canon is that the convalidation must be made in the simple manner. The phrase, *pro convalidatione,* refers only to simple convalidation. There is no indication that the canon includes in its generous concession the power to grant a *sanatio in radice.* On the contrary the sense and prescriptions of the cannon militate against such an interpreta-

mission for the Authentic Interpretation of the Code, Nov. 12, 1922—*AAS,* XIV (1922), 662, 663.

[35] *AAS,* XX (1928), 61.

tion. There is no power given to dispense from the renewal of consent and in fact the renewal of consent is demanded because the form of marriage must be observed. The priest who assists does not receive the faculty to dispense from the observance of the form. Since the form requires that the parties to the marriage exchange their consent [36] before the parish priest and the witnesses [37] it is evident that the *sanatio* is definitely excluded from the power granted to the priest who assists at marriage in virtue of this canon. In every case of convalidation therefore included in this canon the party or parties must renew their consent according to the rules of renewal given in the preceding chapters.

Can the powers of this cannon be used if the parties have concealed their impediment at the time of the first marriage? Does bad faith on the part of the persons concerned in the invalid marriage render the use of these powers invalid? The canon does not exclude this case, nor distinguish good faith from bad. Moreover, when there is question of contracting marriage in such circumstances it is not required that the impediment be entirely hidden until the time of the ceremony. It is sufficient if it remain hidden to the pastor or Ordinary until that time.[38] It seems therefore that even if the parties have entered into the invalid marriage with a knowledge of the impediment the powers of this canon can be used (when the other conditions are present) to convalidate their marriage.

The priests who assist at these marriages and who grant the dispensation must notify the Ordinary of the dispensation granted and enter the record of the marriage into the matrimonial register.[39] If he dispenses in the internal forum, but not in the act of confession, he may send notice of the dispensation to the secret archives of the diocese.[40] Otherwise the registration of the convalidated marriage is to be entered according to the ordinary rules. This is not binding of course on the confessor who dispenses in the act of confession. He need not inform anybody—in fact he may not.

[36] Canon 1095, § 1, 3°. [37] Canon 1094.

[38] Decision of the Pontifical Commission for the Authentic Interpretation of the Code, Mar. 1, 1921—*AAS*, XII (1921), 177.

[39] Canons 1046, 1047.

[40] Vermeersch, *Epitome*, II, n. 311.

CHAPTER VIII

EFFECTS OF CONVALIDATION

Article 1

Validity of the Marriage

The first effect of the convalidation is to establish the validity of the marriage as contract, and, if both parties are baptized, as sacrament.[1] It establishes the perpetual and exclusive bond of marriage by which the parties are united to each other,[2] and from which follow all the effects of marriage, namely, the rights (and the corresponding duties) of each party to those acts which are peculiar to the marriage contract.[3] It imposes upon the married parties the duty of educating in the Catholic religion the children born of the marriage whether before or after the convalidation.

If the convalidated marriage is a sacramental marriage, that is, between two baptized people, the grace of the sacrament is conferred at the moment of convalidation provided the parties are in the state of grace; they receive an increase of sanctifying grace and a title to the actual graces necessary for the correct fulfillment of their marital duties.[4] It is expedient and necessary therefore that the parties be in the state of grace at the moment in which they renew consent for it is at that moment when the sacrament is conferred. If they are in the state of sin they will be incapable of the immediate reception of sacramental grace, and will, moreover, be guilty of sacrilege, material or formal, according as they do or do not advert to the fact. However they do, in any event, receive the title to the graces of the sacrament and will receive the graces as

[1] Canon 1012, § 2.

[2] The convalidated marriage becomes absolutely indissoluble only when it is sacramental and consummated after the renewal of consent. Canon 1118.

[3] Canon 1111.

[4] Council of Trent, Sess. XXIV, *De Sacramento Matrimonii,* Can. 1, 5; Canon 1110.

soon as they have removed the obstacle constituted by their state of sin. But even when the parties are not in the state of grace the convalidation ordinarily should not be postponed for this reason alone, for often greater evils follow from the delay of the convalidation.[5]

These effects follow at the moment in which the man and woman, or either of them as the case may demand, renew consent. It is precisely at that moment that the sacrament is conferred. It is not conferred before that time, for example, at the time in which the dispensation is granted. In this respect the simple convalidation differs from the *sanatio* for by the latter dispensation the marriage becomes valid at the moment of the granting of the *sanatio.*[6]

Article 2

Legitimation of Offspring

Canon 1116. Per subsequens matrimonium parentum sive verum sive putativum, sive noviter contractum sive convalidatum, etiam non consummatum, legitima efficitur proles, dummodo parentes habiles extiterint ad matrimonium inter se contrahendum tempore conceptionis, vel praegnationis vel nativitatis.

Canon 1051. Per dispensationem super impedimento dirimente concessam sive ex potestate ordinaria, sive ex potestate delegata per indultum generale, non vero per rescriptum in casibus particularibus, conceditur quoque eo ipso legitimatio prolis, si qua ex iis cum quibus dispensatur iam nata vel concepta fuerit, excepta tamen adulterina et sacrilega.

A second important effect of the convalidation of marriage is the legitimation of children who have been born of the union while it was yet invalid. Legitimacy is the state of those who are born according to law, and is defined as the state of those "who are conceived or born of a valid or putative marriage, unless the parents at the time of the conception were forbidden the use of marriage already con-

[5] Gasparri, *De Matrimonio* (Ed. 1904), n. 1384.

[6] Canon 1138, § 2.

tracted because of solemn religious profession or sacred orders." [7] If the status of the children does not fulfill all the conditions required by this canon they are illegitimate and contract all the effects of illegitimacy. Therefore, very often the children of parents united in an invalid union are not legitimate. But by subsequent convalidation they can under certain circumstances become legitimized.

In considering legitimation as an effect following from the convalidation of an invalid marriage three hypotheses may be discussed: the marriage may have been putatively valid; it may be convalidated without a dispensation; it may need a dispensation to be convalidated. If the children were born of a putative marriage,[8] which is always invalid, they are considered by law as legitimate as a reward for the good faith of the parents. This is true no matter what the cause of the invalidity was.[9]

But if the invalid marriage is not putative, if it has been contracted in bad faith by both parties, the children are not legitimate. In this event they may under certain conditions be legitimized by a subsequent convalidation of the marriage. The extent of the legitimation varies according as the marriage is convalidated with or without the aid of a dispensation. If the marriage can be convalidated merely by the renewal of consent, because, for example, the impediment has disappeared, the legitimation is governed by Canon 1116. It states that by the subsequent marriage of the parents, even if that is only the convalidation of a previous invalid marriage, the offspring become legitimate provided the parents were qualified to contract a valid marriage at the time of the conception, or of the pregnancy, or of the birth. In other words, the children must be "natural," that is, born of those capable of marrying validly at the time of conception, or pregnancy or birth.[10] If the parties were not capable of contracting during these times the children are considered "spurious." Before the Code it was not certain that all classes of spurious children were excluded from the legitimation by

[7] Canon 1114.

[8] "An invalid marriage is called putative, if it is contracted in good faith by at least one of the parties, until both parties become certain of its nullity." Canon 1015, § 4.

[9] S. C. C., *Parisien. Matrimonii*, Dec. 11, 1880—*Thesaurus*, CXXXIX (1880), 626.

[10] Schmalzgrueber, IV, Pars IV, Tit. XVII. n. 5.

subsequent marriage.[11] The canon now makes it certain that all classes of spurious children are excluded and only natural children included. The Church has power to make this law and effect this legitimation because the legitimacy that it gives is juridical and therefore subject to its laws. When it grants such legitimation to children, it does so by a fiction of the law which refers the validity of the marriage back to the time of conception, pregnancy or birth.[12] It requires consequently that the marriage must have been possible at one of these periods.[13] It is not necessary that the parties should have been capable of marriage during the entire period of conception, gestation and birth, but it suffices if they were capable at any time from the conception to the birth.[14] But if the impediment existed during the whole time from conception to birth and ceased only after birth, the child would be considered spurious and therefore not to be legitimized under the rule of canon 1116.[15] For example, a woman whose marriage is invalid because of the impediment of disparity of worship conceives a child. If the child is born before the impediment has been removed it will be spurious; but if it is born after the removal of the impediment it will be natural and therefore can be legitimized by subsequent convalidation of the marriage of the parents.

It is required of course that the convalidation be valid, or at least effect a putative marriage, though it is not demanded that it be consummated after the convalidation. It is not even required that the consummation be possible as is evident from the concession granted by the Church to legitimize children in danger of death to the parents.[16]

It is not required that the parents must convalidate their marriage immediately upon the birth of the child. They may have

[11] Wernz, *Jus Decretalium*, IV, n. 686, note 53.

[12] Sanchez, *De Matrimonio*, III, Disp. XXXXII, n. 2 ss.

[13] Wernz-Vidal, *Jus Canonicum*, V, n. 614.

[14] Payen, *De Matrimonio*, II, 2177, 1.

[15] Cf. Reply of the Commission for the Authentic Interpretation of the Code, Dec. 6, 1930—*AAS*, XXIII (1931), 25. A child born while the parents were under the impediment of age or disparity of worship although it had ceased at the time of the marriage was declared not legitimized by the subsequent marriage of the parents.

[16] Canon 1043; Schmalzgrueber, IV, Pars IV, Tit. XVIII, n. 50.

postponed it for years, and the case is not infrequent in which the parents have cohabited for many years and finally convalidate their union only in danger of death. This is the case particularly with disparate marriages. Even should the parents separate or obtain a civil divorce, or refuse to renew consent, the children are legitimized if afterwards the parents convalidate their marriage.[17]

Underlying this generous concession of the law is the benefit it is calculated to bring to the children. By it they escape the stigma attached to the faults of their parents, and they obtain a claim to all the rights possessed by legitimate children, except those from which they are expressly barred by the law.[18] A further reason for the concession is found in the hope that the parents may be drawn to convalidate their marriage by the love of the children born to them, realizing the benefits it will confer upon their offspring.[19]

The legitimation is effected by the very fact of marriage regardless of the will of the parents or the children. Even if they wish to exclude the legitimation, it is nevertheless effected in spite of their adverse will. The reason for this is that the concession of the law is granted not merely for the sake of the children and the parents, but also in favor of the marriage itself, and for the public good.[20]

But since the necessity of convalidating marriage frequently arises from the existence of a diriment impediment it follows that many illegitimate children cannot be legitimized merely by subsequent convalidation. In other words, children born of invalid unions are frequently not natural but spurious. In that case they can be legitimized by the second canon quoted. It states that when a dispensation is granted from a diriment impediment by one who

[17] Cappello, *De Sacramentis*, III, n. 750, 5.

[18] Schmalzgrueber, IV, Pars. IV, Tit. XVII, n. 49; Canon 1117. The exceptions mentioned in the law disqualify these children from becoming Cardinals (Canon 232, § 2, 1°), Bishops (Canon 331, § 1, 1°), and Prelates and Abbots Nullius (Canon 320, § 2). A reply of the Commission for the Authentic Interpretation of the Code, July 13, 1930 (*AAS*, XXII [1930], 365, III), states that sons who are legitimized by the subsequent marriage of their parents are regarded as legitimate for admission to the seminary.

[19] Schmalzgrueber, *loc. cit.*

[20] Schmalzgrueber, IV, Pars IV, Tit. XVIII, n. 73; Gasparri, *De Matrimonio* (Ed. 1904), n. 1388.

has the ordinary power to grant it, or one who grants it in virtue of power delegated by a general indult, the children, by the very fact of the granting of a dispensation, are legitimized, except if they are adulterine or sacrilegious. If therefore children are born to persons living in a marriage invalid because of an impediment the children are legitimized when a dispensation is granted with a view to convalidate the marriage, subject to the limitations stated in the canon. The first limitation is that the dispensation must be granted by one who has ordinary power or who has a general indult to grant dispensations.[21] But a dispensation which is granted in virtue of faculties received in a particular rescript does not effect legitimation unless the rescript expressly grants the power to legitimize. Thus if a confessor should ask and obtain from the Sacred Penitentiary the faculty to dispense from an occult impediment for this particular marriage, the children will not be legitimized merely by the fact that in virtue of this faculty a dispensation has been granted. On the contrary, every dispensation granted by the Holy See and those granted by the Ordinary or the priest who assists at a marriage in the circumstances described in Canons 1043, 1044, and 1045, always effects the legitimation of the illegitimate children. The powers granted by these canons are ordinary powers. If a bishop should receive from the Holy See a general indult to dispense from the impediment of consanguinity any dispensation he grants in virtue of that indult legitimizes the children already born by the very fact that the dispensation is granted.[22] The

[21] Canons 197, § 1; 66, § 1.

[22] Thus the power of dispensing which Ordinaries receive in their quinquennial faculties usually will have this same effect. Therefore in the United States legitimation follows when Ordinaries in virtue of their quinquennial faculties and according to the conditions imposed dispense from disparity of worship or from the impediments of minor degree for a just and reasonable cause; from consanguinity in the second or third degree reaching first or in the second degree of the collateral line, from affinity in the first degree of the collateral line either single or when mixed with the second degree, from public propriety in the first degree, when there is a grave and urgent reason for these dispensations and when the marriage cannot be postponed without danger until such dispensation has been obtained from the Holy See. Bouscaren, Quinquennial Faculties—*The Canon Law Digest, Cumulative Supplement*, 1935-1936, pp. 4, 5, 7.

legitimation is granted implicitly by the dispensation.[23] There is no need even to mention the fact of legitimizing in the dispensation; the effect is obtained by the very fact that it has been granted. Before the Code it was necessary even in this class of dispensations to make explicit mention of the legitimation of the children.[24] It is not necessary that the petitioner ask for the legitimation; even if he does not desire it, the children become legitimate and that as soon as the dispensation is executed.[25]

Another limitation excludes the legitimation of adulterine or sacrilegious offspring. Adulterine children are those conceived of parents who are prevented from marrying by the impediment of *ligamen*; sacrilegious, those conceived of parents one at least of whom is in sacred orders or is bound by solemn religious profession. Under such circumstances the children born are not legitimized by a dispensation granted in accord with the prescriptions of Canon 1051. They need a special rescript of legitimation. The canon does not, however, exclude incestuous children from the favor it grants. Therefore children born of parents whose union is invalid because of the impediment of consanguinity in the collateral line are legitimized if a dispensation from the impediment is granted according to the conditions stipulated in the canon.[26] It may be added that the legitimation of children is a valid cause for asking such a dispensation.[27]

It is important to note the difference between the simple convalidation and the *sanatio* in their effect upon the legitimation of children. The difference is noticed only in those marriages which are known to be invalid, for if the marriage is putative the children have no need of legitimation.[28] The first difference is one to time. In the simple convalidation the children become legitimate only from the time of the renewal of consent. In the *sanatio,* they become legitimate from the time of the first ceremony of marriage; by a fiction of law they are considered to have been born of a marriage valid from the very beginning. The second difference is

[23] Chelodi, *Jus Matrimoniale,* n. 49.

[24] Wernz, *Jus Decretalium,* IV, n. 687.

[25] Cappello, *De Sacramentis,* III, n. 291, 7.

[26] Payen, *De Matrimonio,* I, 710, 5.

[27] S. C. de Prop. Fid., *Instructio,* May 9, 1877, ad 8—*Coll.,* n. 1470.

[28] Canon 1114.

one of extent. The *sanatio* legitimizes all the children born of the invalid marriage even those that are spurious; that does not however include those that are adulterine or sacrilegious, or (for a stronger reason) those that are nefarious.[29] In simple convalidation only natural offspring are legitimized if the convalidation is effected merely by a subsequent renewal of consent; if with the aid of a dispensation granted according to the terms of Canon 1051, then the spurious, except the adulterine, sacrilegious and nefarious children are legitimized, but this is in virtue of the dispensation rather than of the convalidation.

[29] S. C. S. Off., July 8, 1903—*Coll.*, n. 2171.

CHAPTER IX

CONVALIDATION IN AMERICAN CIVIL LAW

A consideration of American Civil Law assumes practical importance in the question of convalidation of marriages of unbaptized persons. The Church law of convalidation as previously explained governs only the marriages of all baptized persons, Catholics and non-Catholics. But it does not purport to regulate the marriages of those "who are without," those who are not baptized. Over them it possesses no direct jurisdiction. Consequently their marriages will be regulated by the laws of the civil government to which they are subject, in so far as these laws are just, reasonable and not contrary to divine law.[1] Although this opinion is not beyond dispute it is supported by so many able canonists that it becomes practically certain.[2] It has the support too of many declarations of the Holy See.[3] Consequently it is in the light of the civil law of their respective jurisdiction that the marriages of unbaptized persons must be judged. Two aspects are to be considered; first, the validity of the marriage, and second, the convalidation.

There is no Federal law of marriage as such. To be sure there is Federal legislation governing the Federal jurisdictions such as the District of Columbia and other federal territories. Marriage legislation is subject to the power of the individual state. Attempts to enact uniform marriage legislation for these jurisdictions have been singularly unsuccessful. The result is a variety of state mar-

[1] They are bound to observe also the requirements of natural law. In the event of conflict between the natural law and the civil law of any jurisdiction the natural law prevails.

[2] Schmalzgrueber, IV, Tit. I, n. 367; Gasparri, *De Matrimonio* (Ed. 1932), n. 240; Cappello, *De Sacramentis*, III, n. 75; Vlaming, *Praelectiones Juris Matrimonii*, n. 51; Payen, *De Matrimonio*, I, n. 204.

[3] S. C. Fide, *Instructio*, Dec. 5, 1631—*Coll.*, n. 71; *Tunk. Occid.*, June 26, 1820—*Coll.*, n. 744; S. C. S. Off., *Yun-Nan*, Sept. 20, 1854—*Coll.*, n. 1104; *Coreae*, Sept. 12, 1855, ad 2—*Coll.*, n. 1118; *Natal.*, July 11, 1866—*Fontes*, 996; *Siam*, Nov. 22, 1871, *ad postremum*—*Fontes*, n. 1019; *Niger*, Aug. 17, 1898—*Fontes*, 1205. In the last declaration it is maintained that the form prescribed by civil law must be observed.

riage laws and the necessity of determining the validity of a marriage by an examination of legislation and judicial precedent. But the following conclusions and statements taken from the laws which govern civil marriage may be taken as a guide for the generality of jurisdictions.

It may be stated there are few impediments of civil law which actually render a marriage *invalid* or *void.* The majority of them, together with defects which prevent "real consent," render the marriage only *voidable.* This concept of "voidable" marriage complicates the situation still further. Such a marriage is unknown to Canon Law. It is in direct conflict with the entire notion of the marriage contract and its essential quality of perpetuity which are zealously guarded by Canon Law. By creating a "voidable" marriage civil law gives legal sanction to a status in which one or both parties have the right to void the marriage. Until this is done however the marriage is considered valid. Civil law rejects the theory that a voidable marriage is an invalid marriage until it is later ratified. It adopts the opposite theory that the marriage is valid until it is disaffirmed. Thus if a second marriage were contracted during the existence of a voidable marriage the party attempting this second marriage would be guilty of bigamy and the second marriage would be null due to the impediment of prior marriage.[4] It cannot be said therefore that these marriages are validated later, for they are already considered valid. However it may be noticed that they become absolutely "valid" and no longer "voidable" by subsequent cohabitation of the parties as husband and wife after the condition which rendered them voidable has ceased to exist.[5] This rule may be applied, for example, to youthful persons who lacking the required age of consent can contract only a voidable marriage; it becomes valid, in the absence of avoidance, if the parties live as husband and wife after the age of consent has been attained. The same may be said of some marriages which when first contracted are absolutely void because of other impediments such as prior marriage. In general the courts are inclined to consider them ratified if the parties live together with the inten-

[4] *Ruling Case Law,* XVIII, "Marriage," n. 78; Madden, *Personal and Domestic Relations,* p. 31.

[5] *Ruling Case Law,* XVIII, "Marriage," n. 70; 113 Minn. 503.

tion of cohabiting as husband and wife after the impediment has disappeared.[6] Thus a marriage that has been absolutely void from the impediment of nonage may be validated absolutely when the age of consent has been reached and cohabitation established as an affirmation of their assent to the marriage.[7] But where parties have actually contracted a marriage in good faith that is, without knowledge of the impediment which invalidated their union, after the removal of the impediment a new agreement is not necessary; the marriage becomes valid with the removal of the disability.[8]

This ratification of marriages in civil law may be effected either by statutory provision or by cohabitation and common-law marriages in those states in which they are recognized. As to the former it is a well determined principle of law that the Legislature is supreme in the regulation of marriage law and discipline,[9] and therefore it has the power to ratify and to confirm by statute marriages that were voidable or void because of a disability whose origin is a statute or because they lacked a statutory requirement.[10] In this regard it may be noted that twenty-eight states have curative acts which effect the validation of marriages which might be invalid or at least of doubtful validity.[11] Common law marriages [12] it is generally agreed validate marriages that have been void, if the impediment to the previous invalid union has been removed.[13] This is true only of those states that recognize common law marriages. But it is also true that a marriage which is invalid according to the laws of one state may be validated by the recognition of common-

[6] *Ruling Case Law*, XVIII, "Marriage," n. 70.

[7] *Corpus Juris*, XXXVIII, "Marriage," § 13.

[8] 27 *Harvard L. R.* 380.

[9] Bishop, *Marriage, Divorce and Separation*, § 824.

[10] Madden, *Personal and Domestic Relations*, p. 47; Bishop, *Marriage, Divorce and Separation*, §§ 817, 819. Thus by a law in 1841 the State of Texas ratified marriages that had been invalid because they lacked the proper form. Kent, *Commentary on American Law*, II, n. 204.

[11] Vernier, *American Family Laws*, I, p. 80.

[12] A common law marriage is a marriage that is contracted by the mutual consent of two parties otherwise capable of a valid marriage by an agreement to become husband and wife *per verba de praesenti*. Jacobs, *Cases on Domestic Relations*, p. 377, note 29; 40 W. Va. L. Quart. 78.

[13] 34 *Harvard L. R.* 562; Sims v. Sims, 85 So. (Miss.), 73; *Corpus Juris*, XXXVIII, "Marriage," 96.

law marriages in another if the parties cohabit in the second state and thus form a common-law marriage. In turn this marriage will be recognized as valid by the first state.[14] These are in general the regulations that govern validation in civil law. It will be well to consider each civil incapacity and disability in itself.

1—*Form.* Several states prescribe certain formalities and ceremonies for the celebration of marriage, such as the presence of a minister of religion or civil officer. But the mere legislative requirement does not render the marriage invalid if it is contracted without the proper form. Such an informal marriage is invalid only where the law so provides. Generally speaking provisions relative to the formalities for marriage are deemed regulatory and a violation of such provisions does not render the marriage invalid. A general provision of most states provides that a marriage that is contracted before a person who is not legally authorized to be an official witness but who pretends to be such shall not be invalid because of this defect, and if the marriage is consummated by the parties with belief that they are married the marriage itself becomes valid.[15] In this connection it may be stated that certain jurisdictions have statutes which validate marriages that were contracted after the issuance of licence by one who was not authorized to issue it or if the license was issued in a manner contrary to the law.[16]

2—*Consent.* The three principal defects which prevent "real consent" under civil law are (a) mistake about the identity of the other party or the nature of marriage or its legal consequences; (b) duress or coercion; (c) fraud. In all these cases the marriage is rendered *not void but merely voidable.* Such marriages can be voided by court proceedings instituted by the person who was mistaken, or coerced or deceived.[17] Avoidance cannot take place

[14] 205 U. S. 423, Travers v. Reinhardt, 1907. There are but three jurisdictions which declare in explicit terms that common law marriages are null and void. Besides these three sixteen others are generally considered to hold these common law unions invalid. But twenty-two seem to consider them valid and in the remaining ten jurisdictions it is doubtful whether they are valid. Vernier, *American Family Laws*, p. 104.

[15] Vernier, *American Family Laws*, I, p. 98. Only twenty-three states legislate a form for marriage and these do not require a particular form.

[16] Vernier, *American Family Laws*, I, p. 80.

[17] Madden, *Personal and Domestic Relations*, p. 9; *Ruling Case Law*, XVIII, "Marriage," n. 76.

if the marriage has been consummated by cohabitation or coition, with the knowledge of the alleged fraud.[18]

3—*Impediments.* (a) *Mental Incapacity.* At common law insanity or excessive intoxication, if it incapacitates the mind for deliberate and intelligent consent renders the marriage absolutely null.[19] But in most jurisdictions such marriages are merely voidable by statute; in others they are voidable even in the absence of statute.[20] The tendency in law now is to make these marriages merely voidable, and to be avoided only by judicial decree of annulment.[21] However if one party marries another whom he knows to be insane the marriage may or may not be valid according to the law of the jurisdiction wherein it is contracted. But even if the marriage is absolutely void, in most jurisdictions it may be ratified by marital acts and conduct during a lucid interval.[22] This seems to be true even in those jurisdictions which did not recognize common law marriages.[23]

(b) *Physical incapacity* (impotency). This impediment renders the marriage merely voidable.[24]

(c) *Consanguinity.* Except within the "Levitical degrees" (closer than first cousins) the marriage is voidable in most American jurisdictions.[25]

(d) *Affinity.* Only twenty-five jurisdictions have laws to regulate the impediment of affinity; they make it voidable. Affinity as an impediment in civil law is restricted to the close degrees of relationship. The trend in law is to restrict it further and to abolish it altogether.[26]

[18] *Corpus Juris,* XXXVIII, "Marriage," §§ 61, 70; 42 Ohio State 23, Holz v. Dick.

[19] 25 *Yale Law Journal* 58, 61 (1915).

[20] *Corpus Juris,* XXXVIII, "Marriage," 12; 27 *Columbia Law Review* 845.

[21] Madden, *Personal and Domestic Relations,* p. 27.

[22] Jacobs, *Cases on Domestic Relations,* p. 214.

[23] *Ruling Case Law,* XVIII, "Marriage," n. 78.

[24] *Corpus Juris,* XXXVIII, "Marriage," § 18; Madden, *Personal and Domestic Relations,* p. 36.

[25] *Ruling Case Law,* XVIII, "Marriage," n. 74.

[26] Vernier, *American Family Laws,* I, p. 173; *Corpus Juris,* XXXVIII, "Marriage," § 35.

(e) *Civil incapacity,* i. e., color, race, etc. Usually by statute these marriages are null and void.[27]

(f) *Nonage.* Below the age of seven, all marriages are absolutely void; between seven and the statutory age of consent the marriage is voidable only.[28]

(g) *Prior Marriage.* A prior marriage makes a subsequent marriage absolutely null and void from the beginning. In the event that a second marriage is contracted, three suppositions may be considered. *First,* both parties may be in bad faith. In this case the second marriage is null and remains so. Even if the first marriage is dissolved by divorce or by death, the second remains null because it is presumed to continue as it began, a meretricious union.[29] *Second,* both parties may be in good faith, they believe that they are both free to marry. In this case the marriage becomes valid as soon as the disability resulting from the former marriage disappears, provided of course that the parties continue to cohabit.[30] The reason for this validation is that the parties are presumed to desire the validation and to effect a valid common law marriage.[31] An actual example is that of a man *A* who marries *B* who had already been married to *C*. *B* believes that *C* is dead, and *A* is ignorant entirely of *B*'s former marriage. Later *C* actually died. *A* and *B* continue to cohabit and only later discover the true facts of the case. By that time the marriage had become validated for by the very fact that the disability had disappeared their union was validated by law.[32] *Third.* If only one of the parties is in good faith, the majority of authorities are inclined to say that the marriage becomes validated by a common

[27] Madden, *Personal and Domestic Relations,* p. 38; Vernier, *American Family Laws,* p. 204, says this is true in twenty-six states.

[28] This age of consent varies in the different jurisdictions; usually it is eighteen for males and sixteen for females. Vernier, *American Family Laws,* p. 187; *Ruling Case Law,* XVIII, "Marriage," n. 70.

[29] 21 *Va. L. R.* 331—2 Ja '35.

[30] *Ruling Case Law,* XVIII, "Marriage," n. 78. It is possible that this effect may not be produced in those states that have the requirement of a formal ceremony or a written contract. *Corpus Juris,* XXXVIII, "Marriage," § 96.

[31] 26 *Yale L. R.* 145.

[32] Madden, *Personal and Domestic Relations,* p. 42.

law union after the impediment has disappeared. Others maintain that it does not become valid.[34] An odd angle to this sort of validation is the case of a marriage which though not recognized as valid in one jurisdiction will be recognized as valid there if the parties validate it in a state where that validation is allowed. Thus a man and woman both in good faith married in the state of New York believing that a divorce secured from a former marriage allowed them to contract another marriage. In reality the marriage was invalid because the laws of New York did not recognize the validity of the divorce. They moved later to Illinois in which state the divorce was considered valid, and there they convalidated the second marriage, by a common law marriage. This second marriage is recognized as valid also in other states.[34]

It is important in the convalidation of marriages which are null because of a prior marriage that there be good faith in at least one of the parties, otherwise the second marriages are not ratified by common law marriages.

Civil law therefore admits the validation of marriage. But since there are few incapacities that render a marriage invalid, it can be seen that there are few situations in which civil law convalidates. But when it does convalidate it makes the marriage binding and irrevocable and produces all the civil effects of marriage. This is so especially with regard to the legitimacy of the children. Practically all acts which legalize marriages formerly void, legitimize the children of the marriage. This has practical importance in the question of inheritance of property.[35] In conclusion it may be repeated that it is of vital importance to examine both natural law and civil law of convalidation. In the event of conflict the former overrules the latter.

[33] 4 *Va. L. R.* 326; 24 *Harvard L. R.* 157.

[34] 27 *Harvard L. R.* 380. Conflicts in the marriage laws of the different jurisdictions sometimes make necessary an inquiry into the law of the place wherein the marriage was contracted, the place of the domicile and residence of the parties.

[35] Schouler, *Domestic Relations*, § 228; Vernier, *American Family Laws*, p. 80.

BIBLIOGRAPHY

SOURCES

Acta Apostolicae Sedis (*AAS*), Romae, 1909.
Acta Sanctae Sedis (*ASS*), 41 vols., Romae, 1865-1908.
Canones et Decreta Concilii Tridentini, 19 ed., Taurini, 1913.
Codex Juris Canonici Pii X Pontificis Maximi jussu digestus Benedicti Papae XV auctoritate promulgatus, Romae, 1918.
Codicis Juris Canonici Fontes, cura Emi Petri Car. Gasparri editi, 7 vols., Romae, 1923-1933.
Collectanae S. Congregationis de Propaganda Fide, 2 vols., Romae, 1907.
Corpus Juris Canonici, Editio Lipsiensis II (Richter-Friedberg), 2 vols., Lipsiae, 1922.
Corpus Juris Civiliis, 3 vols., ed. P. Krueger, Berolini, 1928-1929.
Harduin, J., *Conciliorum Collectio Regia Maxima*, 12 vols., Parisiis, 1714-1715.
Jaffe, Philippus, *Regesta Pontificum Romanorum*, 2 Ed., Lipsiae, 1881.
Mansi, Joannes, *Sacrorum Conciliorum Nova et Amplissima Collectio*, 53 vols., Parisiis, 1901-1927.
Pallottini, Salvator, *Collectio Omnium Conclusionum et Resolutionum quae in causis propositis apud S. Cong. Cardinalium S. Concilii Tridentini Interpretum prodierunt ab anno 1564 ad annum 1860*, 17 vols., Romae, 1868-1893.
Richter, Aemilius, *Canones et Decreta Concilii Tridentini*, Lipsiae, 1853.
S. Romanae Rotae Decisiones seu Sententia, Romae, 1909—.
Thesaurus Resolutionum Sacrae Congregationis Concilii, 167 vols., Romae, 1718-1908.

AUTHORS

Alphonsus, De Liguori, *Theologia Moralis*, 5 vols., Taurini, 1872.
Avernus, Gulielmus, *De Sacramentis*, Norimbergae, 1497.
Ayrinhac-Lydon, *Marriage Legislation in New Code of Canon Law*, Revised Edition, New York, Benziger Bros., 1933.
(Bachofen), Charles Augustine, *A Commentary on the New Code of Canon Law*, 4 ed., 8 vols., St. Louis, 1918-1929.
Ballerini, Antonius-Palmieri, Dominicus, *Opus Theologicum Morale*, 7 vols., Prati, 1889.
Bangen, Joannes, *De Sponsalibus et Matrimonio*, 4 vols., Aschendorffia, 1858-1860.
Bassibey, R., *Le Mariage*, Paris, 1899.
Bartolus, *Commentaria*, Venetiis, 1590.
Benedictus XIV, *Opera Omnia*, 17 vols., Prati, 1839-1847.

Bishop, Joel, *Marriage, Divorce and Separation*, Chicago, 1891.
Brillaud, *Traite des Empechements et de Dispenses de Mariage*, Paris, 1871.
Brunnemanus, Joannes, *Commentarius in Codicem Justinianeum*, Lipsiae, 1699.
Brys, J., *De Dispensatione in Jure Canonico*, Brugis, 1925.
Buckland, W. W., *A Text-Book of Roman Law*, Cambridge, 1922.
———, *A Manual of Roman Private Law*, Cambridge, 1925.
Caillaud, *Manuel des Dispenses*, 4th Edition, Paris, 1873.
Cappello, Felix M., *Tractatus Canonico-Moralis De Sacramentis*, Vol. III, *De Matrimonio*, 2 ed., 1933.
Carriere, *Praelectiones Theologicae de Matrimonio*, 2 vols., Paris, 1837.
Cicognani, Amleto (Brennan-O'Hara), *Canon Law*, Philadelphia, 1934.
Clark, E. C., *Roman Private Law*, Cambridge, 1919.
Corbett, Percy E., *The Roman Law of Marriage*, Oxford, 1930.
Corpus Juris, Edited by Wm. McKinney and Burdett Rich, 28 vols.
Creagh, John T., *A Commentary on the Decree Ne Temere*, Baltimore, 1908.
D'Annibale, Josephus, *Summula Theologiae Moralis*, 3 ed., 3 vols., Romae, 1892.
De Becker, Julius, *De Sponsalibus Et Matrimonio Praelectiones Canonicae*, 2 ed., Lovanii, 1903.
Declareuil-Parker, *Rome, The Lawgiver*, New York, 1926.
De Smet, Aloysius, *Betrothment and Marriage*, trans. by A. Owens, 2 ed., 2 vols., St. Louis, 1925.
Dictionnaire de Théologie Catholique, 18 vols., Paris, 1903-1927.
Esmein, A., *Le Mariage en Droit Canonique*, 2 ed., 2 vols., Paris, 1935.
Farrugia, Nicolaus, *De Matrimonio et Causis Matrimonialibus, tractatus canonico-moralis juxta Codicem Juris Canonici*, Romae, 1924.
Feije, Henricus, *De Impedimentis et Dispensationibus Matrimonialibus*, 3 ed., Lovanii, 1885.
Fowler, W. Warde, *Social Life at Rome*, London, 1929.
Freisen, *Geschichte des canonischen Eherechts*, 2 ed., Paderborn, 1893.
Funk, F. X., *Manual of Church History*, trans. by Luigi Cappadelta, 2 vols., London, 1910.
Gasparri, Petrus, *Tractatus Canonicus de Matrimonio*, 3 ed., 2 vols., Parisiis, 1900-1904.
———, *Tractatus Canonicus de Matrimonio* Editio Nova, 2 vols., 1932.
Giovine, *De Dispensationibus Matrimonialibus*, 2 vols., Naples, 1863.
Girard, *Manuel Elementaire de Droit Romain*, 7 ed., Paris, 1924.
Hefele, C., *Conciliengeschichte*, 2 ed., 9 vols., Freiburg, 1873-1890.
Heiss, M., *De Matrimonio*, Monachii, 1861.
Jacobs, Albert, *Cases on Domestic Relations*, Chicago, 1933.
Joannes de Ausbrack, *Summa*, Augustae, 1469.
Kent, James, *Commentary on American Law*, 1830.
Klee, *Die Ehe*, Mainz, 1835.
Laymann, Paulus, *Theologia Moralis*, Venetiis, 1719.

Leage, R. W., *Roman Private Law*, London, 1924.
Lehmkuhl, Augustinus, *Theologia Moralis*, 12 ed., 2 vols., Friburgi Brisgoviae, 1914.
Leitner, Martin, *Lehrbuch des katholischen Eherechts*, 3 ed., Paderborn, 1920.
Madden, Joseph, *Personal and Domestic Relations*, St. Paul, 1931.
Michael de Dalen, *Casus Summarii Decretalium Sexti et Clementini*, Basel, 1479.
Muirhead, James, *Law of Rome*, 3rd ed., London, 1916.
Ojetti, B., *Commentarium in Codicem Juris Canonici*, Romae, 1929.
Palmieri, Dominicus, *Tractatus de Matrimonio Christiano*, Rome, 1890.
Paulus, Florentinus, *Breviarium Juris Canonici*, 1499.
Perrone, Joannes, *De Matrimonio Christiano*, 2 vols., Leodii, 1861.
Petrovits, Joseph, *The New Church Law on Matrimony*, Philadelphia, 1921.
Pichler, Vitus, *Jus Canonicum*, 2 vols., Ravennae, 1741.
Pirhing, Enricus, *Jus Canonicum Nova Methodo Explicatum*, 2 vols., Delingae, 1678.
Pruemmer, M., *Manuale Theologiae Moralis*, 3 ed., 3 vols., Friburgi, 1928.
Rigantius, *Commentaria in Regulas*, Coloniae Allobrogum, 4 vols., 1751.
Reiffenstuel, Anacletus, *Jus Canonicum Universum*, 4 vols., Romae, 1838.
Repertorium aureum super toto corpore Juris Canonici, Cologne, 1475.
Roby, Henry J., *Roman Private Law*, 2 vols., Cambridge, 1902.
Sanchez, Thomas, *De Sancto Matrimonii Sacramento Disputationum*, Tomi Tres, Lugduni, 1669.
Scherer, R., *Handbuch des Kirchenrechts*, 2 vols., Graz, 1886.
Schmalzgrueber, Franciscus, *Jus Ecclesiasticum*, 12 vols., Rome, 1844.
Schouler, James, *Domestic Relations*, Chicago, 1882.
Stiegler, Maria, *Dispensation, Dispensationswesen, und Dispensationsrecht*, Mainz, 1901.
Tanquerey, Ad., *Synopsis Theologiae Moralis*, 8 ed., 3 vols., Rome, 1921.
Van Espen, Z. B., *Jus Ecclesiasticum Universum*, 5 vols., Lugduni, 1778.
Vecchiotti, Septimus, *Tractatus Canonicus de Matrimonio*, 3 vols., Augustae Taurinorum, 1876.
Vermeersch, A.-Creusen, J., *Epitome Juris Canonici*, 3 ed., 3 vols., Mechliniae, 1927.
Vernier, Chester, *American Family Laws*, Stanford Univ., 1931-1935.
Vidal, Petrus, *Institutiones Juris Civilis Romani*, Prati, 1915.
Vlaming, Th. M., *Praelectiones Juris Matrimonii*, 3 ed., 2 vols., Bussum in Hollandia, 1921.
Voet, J., *Commentarium ad Pandectas*, 8 vols., Bassoni, 1827.
Vocabularium Utriusque Juris, Strassburg, 1486.
Wernz, F. X., *Jus Decretalium*, 2 ed., 6 vols., Prati, 1912.
Wernz-Vidal, Petrus, *Jus Canonicum ad Codicis Norman Exactum*, 5 vols., Vol. V, *Jus Matrimoniale*, Romane, 1923-1928.
Woywod, Stanislaus, *A Practical Commentary on the Code of Canon Law*, 2 vols., New York, 1925.

Zaberella, Francisco, *Lectura super Clementinis*, Turin, 1492.
Zitelli, Seph., *De Dispensationibus Matrimonialibus*, Rome, 1887.
de Zocchis, Jacobus, *Canon Omnis Utriusque Juris*, Padua, 1472.

Periodicals

American Ecclesiastical Review (*AER*), Philadelphia, 1889—.
Appolinaris, Rome, 1928—.
Archiv fuer katholisches Kirchenrecht, Mainz, 1857—.
Collationes Brugenses, Brugis, 1895—.
Harvard Law Review, Cambridge, 1887—.
Irish Ecclesiastical Record (*IER*), Dublin, 1864—.
Periodica de Re Canonica et Morali, Brugis, 1905—; ab anno 1927: *Periodica de Re Canonica, Morali, Liturgica.*
Zeitschrift der Savigny-Stiftung fuer Rechtsgeschichte, Weimar, 1880—.

ALPHABETICAL INDEX

BIOGRAPHICAL NOTE

James H. Brennan was born on June 7, 1905, at Branch Dale, Pa. After receiving his elementary education in the public school there he entered St. Francis College, Loretto, Pa., and received the degree of Bachelor of Arts in 1927. In the fall of the same year he began his theological studies in St. Mary's Seminary, Baltimore, Md. During the course of these studies he received the degree of Master of Arts in June, 1928, and that of Bachelor of Sacred Theology in June, 1930. He was ordained to the sacred priesthood on June 11, 1931. In June of the following year he was admitted to the Society of Saint Sulpice. In 1934 he entered the Gregorian University at Rome for post-graduate studies in Canon Law. The degree of Bachelor of Canon Law was conferred on him in 1935. He transferred to the School of Canon Law at the Catholic University of America, Washington, D. C., and here received the Licentiate in Canon Law in 1936.

CANON LAW STUDIES

1. FRERIKS, REV. CELESTINE A., C.PP.S., J.C.D., Religious Congregations in Their External Relations, 121 pp., 1916.
2. GALLIHER, REV. DANIEL M., O.P., J.C.D., Canonical Elections, 117 pp., 1917.
3. BORKOWSKI, REV. AURELIUS L., O.F.M., J.C.D., De Confraternitatibus Ecclesiasticis, 136 pp., 1918.
4. CASTILLO, REV. CAYO, J.C.D., Disertacion Historico-Canonica sobre la Potestad del Cabildo en Sede Vacante o Impedida del Vicario Capitular, 99 pp., 1919 (1918).
5. KUBELBECK, REV. WILLIAM J., S.T.B., J.C.D., The Sacred Penitentiaria and Its Relation to Faculties of Ordinaries and Priests, 129 pp., 1918.
6. PETROVITS, REV. JOSEPH, J.C., S.T.D., J.C.D., The New Church Law on Matrimony, X-461 pp., 1919.
7. HICKEY, REV. JOHN J., S.T.B., J.C.D., Irregularities and Simple Impediments in the New Code of Canon Law, 100 pp., 1920.
8. KLEKOTKA, REV. PETER J., S.T.B., J.C.D., Diocesan Consultors, 179 pp., 1920.
9. WANENMACHER, REV. FRANCIS, J.C.D., The Evidence is Ecclesiastical Procedure Affecting the Marriage Bond, 1920 (Printed 1935).
10. GOLDEN, REV. HENRY FRANCIS, J.C.D., Parochial Benefices in the New Code, IV-119 pp., 1921 (Printed 1925).
11. KOUDELKA, REV. CHARLES J., J.C.D., Pastors, Their Rights and Duties According to the New Code of Canon Law, 211 pp., 1921.
12. MELO, REV. ANTONIUS, O.F.M., J.C.D., De Exemptione Regularium, X-188 pp., 1921.
13. SCHAAF, REV. VALENTINE THEODORE, O.F.M., S.T.B., J.C.D., The Cloister, X-180 pp., 1921.
14. BURKE, REV. THOMAS JOSEPH, S.T.D., J.C.D., Competence in Ecclesiastical Tribunals, IV-117 pp., 1922.
15. LEECH, REV. GEORGE LEO, J.C.D., A Comparative Study of the Constitution "Apostolicae Sedis" and the "Codex Juris Canonici," 179 pp., 1922.
16. MOTRY, REV. HUBERT LOUIS, S.T.D., J.C.D., Diocesan Faculties According to the Code of Canon Law, II-167 pp., 1922.
17. MURPHY, REV. GEORGE LAWRENCE, J.C.D., Delinquencies and Penalties in the Administration and the Reception of the Sacraments, IV-121 pp., 1923.
18. O'REILLY, REV. JOHN ANTHONY, S.T.B., J.C.D., Ecclesiastical Sepulture in the New Code of Canon Law, II-129 pp., 1923.
19. MICHALICKA, REV. WENCESLAS CYRILL, O.S.B., J.C.D., Judicial Procedure in Dismissal of Clerical Exempt Religious, 107 pp., 1923.
20. DARGIN, REV. EDWARD VINCENT, S.T.B., J.C.D., Reserved Cases According to the Code of Canon Law, IV-103 pp., 1924.

21. GODFREY, REV. JOHN A., S.T.B., J.C.D., The Right of Patronage According to the Code of Canon Law, 153 pp., 1924.
22. HAGEDORN, REV. FRANCIS EDWARD, J.C.D., General Legislation on Indulgences, II-154 pp., 1924.
23. KING, REV. JAMES IGNATIUS, J.C.D., The Administration of the Sacraments to Dying Non-Catholics, V-141 pp., 1924.
24. WINSLOW, REV. FRANCIS JOSEPH, O.F.M., J.C.D., Vicars and Prefects Apostolic, IV-149 pp., 1924.
25. CORREA, REV. JOSE SERVELION, S.T.L., J.C.D., La Potestad Legislativa de la Iglesia Catolica, IV-127 pp., 1925.
26. DUGAN, REV. HENRY FRANCIS, A.M., J.C.D., The Judiciary Department of the Diocesan Curia, 87 pp., 1925.
27. KELLER, REV. CHARLES FREDERICK, S.T.B., J.C.D., Mass Stipends, 167 pp., 1925.
28. PASCHANG, REV. JOHN LINUS, J.C.D., The Sacramentals According to the Code of Canon Law, 129 pp., 1925.
29. POINTEK, REV. CYRILLUS, O.F.M., S.T.B., J.C.D., De Indulto Exclaustrationis necnon Saecularizationis, XIII-289 pp., 1925.
30. KEARNEY, REV. RICHARD JOSEPH, S.T.B., J.C.D., Sponsors at Baptism According to the Code of Canon Law, IV-127 pp., 1925.
31. BARTLETT, REV. CHESTER JOSEPH, A.M., LL.B., J.C.D., The Tenure of Parochial Property in the United States of America, V-108 pp., 1926.
32. KILKER, REV. ADRIAN JEROME, J.C.D., Extreme Unction, V-425 pp., 1926.
33. MCCORMICK, REV. ROBERT EMMETT, J.C.D., Confessors of Religious, VIII-266 pp., 1926.
34. MILLER, REV. NEWTON THOMAS, J.C.D., Founded Masses According to the Code of Canon Law, VII-93 pp., 1926.
35. ROELKER, REV. EDWARD G., S.T.D., J.C.D., Principles of Privilege According to the Code of Canon Law, XI-166 pp., 1926.
36. BAKALARCZYK, REV. RICHARDUS, M.I.C., J.U.D., De Novitiatu, VIII-208 pp., 1927.
37. PIZZUTI, REV. LAWRENCE, O.F.M., J.U.L., De Parochis Religiosis, 1927. (Not Printed.)
38. BLILEY, REV. NICHOLAS MARTIN, O.S.B., J.C.D., Altars According to the Code of Canon Law, XIX-132 pp., 1927.
39. BROWN, MR. BRENDAN FRANCIS, A.B., LL.M., J.U.D., The Canonical Juristic Personality with Special Reference to its Status in the United States of America, V-212 pp., 1927.
40. CAVANAUGH, REV. WILLIAM THOMAS, C.P., J.U.D., The Reservation of the Blessed Sacrament, VIII-101 pp., 1927.
41. DOHENY, REV. WILLIAM J., C.S.C., A.B., J.U.D., Church Property: Modes of Acquisition, X-118 pp., 1927.
42. FELDHAUS, REV. ALOYSIUS H., C.PP.S., J.C.D., Oratories, IX-141 pp., 1927.
43. KELLY, REV. JAMES PATRICK, A.B., J.C.D., The Jurisdiction of the Simple Confessor, X-208 pp., 1927.

44. NEUBERGER, REV. NICHOLAS J., J.C.D., Canon 6 or the Relation of the Codex Juris Canonici to the Preceding Legislation, V-95 pp., 1927.
45. O'KEEFE, REV. GERALD MICHAEL, J.C.D., Matrimonial Dispensations, Powers of Bishops, Priests, and Confessors, VIII-232 pp., 1927.
46. QUIGLEY, REV. JOSEPH A. M., A.B., J.C.D., Condemned Societies, 139 pp., 1927.
47. ZAPLOTNIK, REV. JOHANNES LEO, J.C.D., De Vicariis Foraneis, X-142 pp., 1927.
48. DUSKIE, REV. JOHN ALOYSIUS, A.B., J.C.D., The Canonical Status of the Orientals in the United States, VIII-196 pp., 1928.
49. HYLAND, REV. FRANCIS EDWARD, J.C.D., Excommunication, Its Nature, Historical Development and Effects, VIII-181 pp., 1928.
50. REINMANN, REV. GERALD JOSEPH, O.M.C., J.C.D., The Third Order Secular of Saint Francis, 201 pp., 1928.
51. SCHENK, REV. FRANCIS J., J.C.D., The Matrimonial Impediments of Mixed Religion and Disparity of Cult, XVI-318 pp., 1929.
52. COADY, REV. JOHN JOSEPH, S.T.D., J.U.D., A.M., The Appointment of Pastors, VIII-150 pp., 1929.
53. KAY, REV. THOMAS HENRY, J.C.D., Competence in Matrimonial Procedure, VIII-164 pp., 1929.
54. TURNER, REV. SIDNEY JOSEPH, C.P., J.U.D., The Vow of Poverty, XLIX-217 pp., 1929.
55. KEARNEY, REV. RAYMOND A., A.B., S.T.D., J.C.D., The Principles of Delegation, VII-149 pp., 1929.
56. CONRAN, REV. EDWARD JAMES, A.B., J.C.D., The Interdict, V-163 pp., 1930.
57. O'NEIL, REV. WILLIAM H., J.C.D., Papal Rescripts of Favor, VII-218 pp., 1930.
58. BASTNAGEL, REV. CLEMENT VINCENT, J.U.D., The Appointment of Parochial Adjutants and Assistants, XV-257 pp., 1930.
59. FERRY, REV. WILLIAM A., A.B., J.C.D., Stole Fees, V-136 pp., 1930.
60. COSTELLO, REV. JOHN MICHAEL, A.B., J.C.D., Domicile and Quasi-Domicile, VII-201 pp., 1930.
61. KREMER, REV. MICHAEL NICHOLAS, A.B., S.T.B., J.C.D., Church Support in the United States, VI-136 pp., 1930.
62. ANGULO, REV. LUIS, C.M., J.C.D., Legislation de la Iglesia sobre la intencion en la application de la Santa Misa, VII-104 pp., 1931.
63. FREY, REV. WOLFGANG NORBERT, O.S.B., A.B., J.C.D., The Act of Religious Profession, VIII-174 pp., 1931.
64. ROBERTS, REV. JAMES BRENDAN, A.B., J.C.D., The Banns of Marriage, XIV-140 pp., 1931.
65. RYDER, REV. RAYMOND ALOYSIUS, A.B., J.C.D., Simony, IX-151 pp., 1931.
66. CAMPAGNA, REV. ANGELO, PH.D., J.U.D., Il Vicario Generale del Vescovo, VII-205 pp., 1931.
67. COX, REV. JOSEPH GODFREY, A.B., J.C.D., The Administration of Seminaries, VI-124 pp., 1931.

68. GREGORY, REV. DONALD J., J.U.D., The Pauline Privilege, XV-165 pp., 1931.
69. DONOHUE, REV. JOHN F., J.C.D., The Impediment of Crime, VII-110 pp., 1931.
70. DOOLEY, REV. EUGENE A., O.M.I., J.C.D., Church Law on Sacred Relics, IX-143 pp., 1931.
71. ORTH, REV. CLEMENT RAYMOND, O.M.C., J.C.D., The Approbation of Religious Institutes, 171 pp., 1931.
72. PERNICONE, REV. JOSEPH M., A.B., J.C.D., The Ecclesiastical Prohibition of Books, XII-267 pp., 1932.
73. CLINTON, REV. CONNELL, A.B., J.C.D., The Paschal Precept, IX-108 pp., 1932.
74. DONNELLY, REV. FRANCIS B., A.M., S.T.L., J.C.D., The Diocesan Synod, VIII-125 pp., 1932.
75. TORRENTE, REV. CAMILO, C.M.F., J.C.D., Las Processiones Sagradas, V-145 pp., 1932.
76. MURPHY, REV. EDWIN J., C.PP. S., J.C.D., Suspension Ex Informata Conscientia, XI-122 pp., 1932.
77. MACKENZIE, REV. ERIC F., A.M., S.T.L., J.C.D., The Delict of Heresy in its Commission, Penalization, Absolution, VII-124 pp., 1932.
78. LYONS, REV. AVITUS E., S.T.B., J.C.D., The Collegiate Tribunal of First Instance, XI-147 pp., 1932.
79. CONNOLLY, REV. THOMAS A., J.C.D., Appeals, XI-195 pp., 1932.
80. SANGMEISTER, REV. JOSEPH V., A.B., J.C.D., Force and Fear as Precluding Matrimonial Consent, V-211 pp., 1932.
81. JAEGER, REV. LEO A., A.B., J.C.D., The Administration of Vacant and Quasi-Vacant Episcopal Sees in the United States, IX-229 pp., 1932.
82. RIMLINGER, REV. HERBERT T., J.C.D., Error Invalidating Matrimonial Consent, VII-79 pp., 1932.
83. BARRETT, REV. JOHN D. M., S.S., J.C.D., A Comparative Study of the Third Plenary Council of Baltimore and the Code, IX-221 pp., 1932.
84. CARBERRY, REV. JOHN J., PH.D., S.T.D., J.C.D., The Juridical Form of Marriage, X-177 pp., 1934.
85. DOLAN, REV. JOHN L., A.B., J.C.D., The Defensor Vinculi, XII-157 pp., 1934.
86. HANNAN, REV. JEROME D., A.M., S.T.D., LL.B., J.C.D., The Canon Law of Wills, IX-517 pp., 1934.
87. LEMIEUX, REV. DELISLE A., A.M., J.C.D., The Sentence in Ecclesiastical Procedure, IX-131 pp., 1934.
88. O'ROURKE, REV. JAMES J., A.B., J.C.D., Parish Registers, VII-109 pp., 1934.
89. TIMLIN, REV. BARTHOLOMEW, O.F.M., A.M., J.C.D., Conditional Matrimonial Consent, X-381 pp., 1934.
90. WAHL, REV. FRANCIS X., A.B., J.C.D., The Matrimonial Impediments of Consanguinity and Affinity, VI-125 pp., 1934.

91. WHITE, REV. ROBERT J., A.B., LL.B., S.T.B., J.C.D., Canonical Ante-Nuptial Promises and the Civil Law, VI-152 pp., 1934.
92. HERRERA, REV. ANTONIO PARRA, O.C.D., J.C.D., Legislation Ecclesiastica sobra el Ayuno y la Abstinencia, XI-191 pp., 1935.
93. KENNEDY, REV. EDWIN J., J.C.D., The Special Matrimonial Process in Cases of Evident Nullity, X-165 pp., 1935.
94. MANNING, REV. JOHN J., A.B., J.C.D., Presumption of Law in Matrimonial Procedure, XI-111 pp., 1935.
95. MOEDER, REV. JOHN M., J.C.D., The Proper Bishop for Ordination and Dimissorial Letters, VII-135 pp., 1935.
96. O'MARA, REV. WILLIAM A., A.B., J.C.D., Canonical Causes for Matrimonial Dispensations, IX-155 pp., 1935.
97. REILLY, REV. PETER, J.C.D., Residence of Pastors, IX-81 pp., 1935.
98. SMITH, REV. MARINER T., O.P., S.T.Lr., J.C.D., The Penal Law for Religious, VII-169 pp., 1935.
99. WHALEN, REV. DONALD W., A.M., J.C.D., The Value of Testimonial Evidence in Matrimonial Procedure, XIII-297 pp., 1935.
100. CLEARY, REV. JOSEPH F., J.C.D., Canonical Limitations on the Alienation of Church Property, VIII-141 pp., 1936.
101. GLYNN, REV. JOHN C., J.C.D., The Promoter of Justice, XX-337 pp., 1936.
102. BRENNAN, REV. JAMES H., S.S., A.M., S.T.B., J.C.L., The Simple Convalidation of Marriage, 1937.
103. BRUNINI, REV. JOSEPH BERNARD, A.B., S.T.B., J.C.L., Clerical Obligations of Canons 139 and 142, 1937.
104. CONNOR, REV. MAURICE, J.C.L., The Administrative Removal of Pastors, 1937.
105. GUILFOYLE, REV. MERLIN JOSEPH, J.C.L., Custom, 1937.
106. HUGHES, REV. JAMES A., A.B., A.M., J.C.L., Witnesses in Criminal Trials of Clerics, 1937.
107. JANSEN, REV. RAYMOND J., Canonical Provisions for Catechetical Instruction, 1937.
108. KEALY, REV. JOHN J., A.B., J.C.L., The Introductory Libellus in the Church Court, 1937.
109. MCMANUS, REV. JAMES EDWARD, C.SS.R., J.C.L., The Administration of Temporal Goods in Religious Institutes, 1937.
110. MORIARITY, REV. EUGENE JAMES, J.C.L., Oaths in Ecclesiastical Courts, 1937.
111. RAINER, REV. ELIGIUS GEORGE, C.SS.R., J.C.L., Suspension of Clerics, 1937.
112. REILLY, REV. THOMAS F., C.SS.R., J.C.L., Visitation of Religious, 1937.

www.ingramcontent.com/pod-product-compliance
Lightning Source LLC
LaVergne TN
LVHW050211080826
844660LV00012B/395

* 9 7 8 0 8 1 3 2 2 2 9 1 2 *